First Steps for Building SAP®UI5 Mobile Apps

Robert Burdwell

Thank you for purchasing this book from Espresso Tutorials!

Like a cup of espresso coffee, Espresso Tutorials SAP books are concise and effective. We know that your time is valuable and we deliver information in a succinct and straightforward manner. It only takes our readers a short amount of time to consume SAP concepts. Our books are well recognized in the industry for leveraging tutorial-style instruction and videos to show you step by step how to successfully work with SAP.

Check out our YouTube channel to watch our videos at
https://www.youtube.com/user/EspressoTutorials.

If you are interested in SAP Finance and Controlling, join us at
http://www.fico-forum.com/forum2/
to get your SAP questions answered and contribute to discussions.

Related titles from Espresso Tutorials:

- ▶ Michal Krawczyk: SAP® SOA Integration – Enterprise Service Monitoring
  http://5077.espresso-tutorials.com
- ▶ Anurag Barua: First Steps in SAP® Fiori
  http://5126.espresso-tutorials.com
- ▶ Paul Bakker & Rick Bakker: How to Pass the SAP® ABAP Certification Exam
  http://5136.espresso-tutorials.com
- ▶ Thomas Stutenbäumer: Practical Guide to ABAP®. Part 2: Performance, Enhancements, Transports
  http://5138.espresso-tutorials.com
- ▶ Bert Vanstechelman: The SAP® HANA Deployment Guide
  http://5171.espresso-tutorials.com
- ▶ Raquel Seville: SAP® OpenUI5 for Mobile BI and Analytics
  http://5173.espresso-tutorials.com

Robert Burdwell
First Steps for Building SAP®UI5 Mobile Apps

ISBN:	978-1-979000-86-4
Editor:	Karen Schoch
Cover Design:	Philip Esch, Martin Munzel
Cover Photo:	fotolia #93200711 © envfx
Interior Design:	Johann-Christian Hanke

All rights reserved.

1st Edition 2017, Gleichen

© 2017 by Espresso Tutorials GmbH

URL: *www.espresso-tutorials.com*

Feedback
We greatly appreciate any kind of feedback you have concerning this book. Please mail us at *info@espresso-tutorials.com*.

Table of Contents

Introduction   9

1 Introduction to Mobile Development   11

  1.1   History of smart phones   11

  1.2   Native or hybrid   12

  1.3   HTML   13

  1.4   CSS   14

  1.5   JavaScript   15

  1.6   XML   16

  1.7   Cordova   18

  1.8   OData   18

2 SAPUI5 Development   21

  2.1   Open UI5   22

  2.2   SAPUI5 Development Toolkit   23

  2.3   ListBox   24

  2.4   SAPUI5 libraries   27

  2.5   Themes   30

3 Model View Controller (MVC)   33

  3.1   HTML Example   35

  3.2   View example   38

  3.3   Model example   39

  3.4   Controller example   41

4 SAPUI5 apps with Eclipse   43

  4.1   Install Eclipse Java Development Kit (JDK)   43

  4.2   SAP development tools   44

  4.3   Push button and text app   49

4.4	SAP Development tools for Eclipse	55
4.5	Create OData web service	57

5 SAP Mobile Platform Server — **61**

5.1	SMP server purchase options	63
5.2	SAP Service Marketplace	64
5.3	SMP Server preparation	66
5.4	Connect Eclipse to SAP Mobile Platform Administration and Monitoring	72
5.5	SMP Server new application	73
5.6	Gateway Management Cockpit	76

6 SAP Mobile Platform SDK — **79**

6.1	SMP SDK for Visual Studio	81

7 SAPUI5 with SAP Cloud Platform — **85**

7.1	Purchase options	85
7.2	Logging into the SAP Cloud Platform	86

8 Building Apps with the SAP Cloud Platform — **95**

8.1	Create app – SAP Cloud Platform	95
8.2	Create app in SAP Web IDE	97
8.3	Layout Editor	106
8.4	Odata app	110
8.5	Create, import, route and deploy app	116
8.6	Git clone app	123
8.7	Delete app	124

9 Building SAPUI5 Apps with Visual Studio — **127**

9.1	New project	128
9.2	Kapsel	135
9.3	Visual Studio market place	140
9.4	Git	141
9.5	OpenUI5-sources	143

10 Resources   145

11 References   146

A The Author   148

B Index   149

C Disclaimer   150

Introduction

This book aims to explore opportunities for building mobile apps with SAPUI5. The platforms covered in this content are *Eclipse*, *SAP Cloud Platform* and *Microsoft Visual Studio*. There's no question mobile device usage has become an integral part of our personal and professional lives. To a degree, these devices dictate how we interact with society, find information and basically function. In the past, we viewed magazines or stared off in into the distance to pass the time; now we catch up on text messages, reply to work emails, browse the internet or play games to pass the time. It is amazing how society has adapted to these technological instruments as a vital part of life. Although entertainment apps have their place in the market, this book will focus on building business and data-driven applications using different platforms to deploy hybrid applications to multiple devices.

The content found in this book will act as a guide to show you the different environments that can be used with SAPUI5. This is extremely beneficial because as developers, you have the option to use your preferred environment for development. You are no longer restricted to using one platform that may pose issues for you.

We have added a few icons to highlight important information. These include:

Tips
Tips highlight information that provides more details about the subject being described and/or additional background information.

Examples

 Examples help illustrate a topic better by relating it to real world scenarios.

Attention

 Attention notices highlight information that you should be aware of when you go through the examples in this book on your own.

Excercises

 Exercises help you to solidify and deepen your knowledge.

Finally, a note concerning the copyright: all screenshots printed in this book are the copyright of SAP SE. All rights are reserved by SAP SE. Copyright pertains to all SAP images in this publication. For the sake of simplicity, we do not mention this specifically underneath every screenshot.

1 Introduction to Mobile Development

Mobile development has dramatically advanced over the past ten years. We started with native development and then slowly matured to opportunities with hybrid and flexible environments. This book will focus on creating mobile apps with SAPUI5 using Eclipse with SAP Mobile Platform (SMP), SAP Cloud Platform and Microsoft Visual Studio. There are numerous mobile apps for fitness, entertainment, socializing, chatting and viewing videos, as well as many other categories. Consumers tend to gravitate to these apps while organizations rely on websites and mobile sites for sales and operations. However, organizations also need mobile app options for their customers, employees and business relationships.

Although these business mobile apps may not be as entertaining, they do serve the purpose of displaying useful information, graphics or analytics to executives, managers and employees in order to make real time, strategic and operational decisions. Information populated into these apps can be derived from Transactional Processing Systems (TPS), Customer Relationship Management (CRM), Supply Chain Management (SCM) and Enterprise Resource Planning (ERP) systems. Business applications can vary in their use in financial, healthcare, retail, manufacturing, human resources, asset management and inventory systems. Utilizing a mobile app to retrieve and interact with data sounds great, but the value of mobile apps is seen in the usage and acceptance by end users.

1.1 History of smart phones

Over forty years ago, Motorola unveiled its first mobile device. We then moved into the 1990s where IBM Simon was the entrant into the smartphone market. While previous phones were rather bulky compared to today's iPhone and Android devices, they provided a framework and acceptance for what we have today. Each day consumers use their mobile phones for communication, internet browsing, gaming, global positioning systems (GPS), social interactions and much more.

It has been stated that billions of mobile phones are currently in use around the world. We have seen mobile application usage double from year to year with billions of yearly downloads. Almost every organization can envision the vast opportunities and revenue generation that are possible from mobile apps in their market.

1.2   Native or hybrid

In the past, developers had to decide whether to develop mobile applications with native environments like *Java for Android*, or *Objective C for IOS*. The development decision process and complexity expanded when debates surfaced on whether to develop using native or hybrid (HTML5, CSS and JavaScript) for mobile development. The issue with native development is that one team of employees is needed to develop for iOS with Xcode and another team to develop Android with Java. This can be costly and less productive because, in this scenario, we have to develop the same app in two different environments as well as manage our websites and mobile sites. An organization's audience for their mobile app becomes a key factor in making development decisions.

As with every business service or product, competition ultimately lowers prices or provides substitutions. However, having numerous vendors in the same vertical market increases complexity and confusion. The mobile development platform has now experienced the same evolution as we have seen with the internet, computers, cloud computing and electronics. We now see many hybrid vendors offering stand-alone or cloud platforms for mobile development, e.g. *Telerik*, *Xamarin*, *Kony*, *Appcelerator*, *Adobe* and many others.

An organization can easily see the benefits of building with a hybrid approach since it offers a better use of resources; however, some hybrid environments lack the essential native features such as maps, voice commands, social integrations, photo sharing, mail and browsing, among many others. It takes time to research the environments, but as with most technological innovations, they become more robust each year. This book focuses on a hybrid approach using HTML5, CSS and JavaScript with SAPUI5 for development. Please see Table 1.1 for a description of native versus hybrid development.

Development	Description
Native	A native app is developed with Objective C for iOS or Java for Android developers.
Hybrid	This is the ability to develop mobile apps using HTML5, JavaScript and CSS, to be deployed on iOS, Android or Windows devices.

Table 1.1: Mobile development – native and hybrid

1.3   HTML

HTML stands for *Hyper Text Markup Language*. It is the official scripting language for the World Wide Web. Many webpages both internal and external have HTML embedded within its pages. Therefore, it is important to learn the basics and foundations of HTML prior to building a mobile application. HTML can be used to create websites, mobile websites and mobile apps.

We recommend that readers of this book understand HTML tags and structure before building a mobile app with SAPUI5. We will be using the Java Developer platform with HTML, CSS and JavaScript.

As you can see in Figure 1.1, the DOCTYPE is 'html' to indicate the page is using Hypertext Markup Language. Additionally, there is a link to the CSS page along with several scripts for JavaScript.

```
<!DOCTYPE html>
<html>
    <head>
    <!--
        Customize the content security policy in the meta
        For details, see http://go.microsoft.com/fwlink/?
    -->
        <meta http-equiv="Content-Security-Policy" conten

        <meta name="format-detection" content="telephone=
        <meta name="msapplication-tap-highlight" content=
        <meta name="viewport" content="user-scalable=no,
        <link rel="stylesheet" type="text/css" href="css/
        <title>htmlexample</title>
    </head>
    <body>
        <div class="app">
            <h1>HTML Code Example </h1>
            <div id="deviceready" class="blink">
                <p class="event listening">Connecting to
                <p class="event received">Device is Ready
            </div>
        </div>
        <script type="text/javascript" src="cordova.js"><
        <script type="text/javascript" src="scripts/platf
        <script type="text/javascript" src="scripts/index
    </body>
</html>
```

Figure 1.1: HTML code example

1.4   CSS

Cascading Style Sheets (CSS) is the method of designing and formatting how fonts or layouts will appear on the page or view. For example, we need a requirement for a list item to appear in the center of the view. In this case, we create a style to position the list group to be centered.

This allows you to set the border, width, height, radius, alignment, padding, font style, font type, etc. It is important to note that most CSS formatting is written in an external CSS page. In the example below, you can review the code to attach an external style sheet to the index.html page. This approach will be used in almost every example throughout this book.

CSS Link example

```
<link rel="stylesheet" type="text/css"
href="styles.css">
```

External CSS tip

CSS can be applied within the body of the html code or attached to the head of the index.html page. Additionally, there are times when you can attach an external CSS URL, but this can cause issues if the external CSS page is updated without your knowledge.

CSS3 is an enhancement and evolution of CSS that provides the flexibility to incorporate gradients, rounded corners, text effects, 2D and 3D transformations and animations. Developers can improve a page and view load times by using CSS3 instead of large jpeg images.

1.5 JavaScript

JavaScript allows windows, buttons, images, pages, objects or text to have interactivity. The JavaScript code can be embedded in the html page or linked to a JavaScript file. Most of the views created with mobile apps will have JavaScript statements used as a content reference to the index page. JavaScript is case sensitive so we have to ensure that the variables are named correctly when using them throughout the application. In addition, JavaScript requires a semicolon for the close of each statement and ignores whitespace in the scripts.

In SAPUI5, we can develop mobile apps using JavaScript, XML, JSON or HTML. Figure 1.2 shows the options when creating an SAPUI5 app; however, this book will focus on using XML structure for the views.

Figure 1.2: Development options

1.6   XML

eXtensible Markup Language (XML) is primarily used for data structures to present data in pages, forms or displays. It is lightweight and can be stored in the file structure of the app. In Figure 1.3, you can see that the Entity Type, Key and Property are used to structure weather data. We will use this XML data structure in Chapter 4 when we connect Eclipse to an XML feed. However, most of the page development with the SAPUI5 tutorials will use a view.xml file to display the content of the page.

As you can see, we can use XML as a data source with our mobile apps, but XML can also be used as a view when building the mobile apps with SAPUI5. Figure 1.4 shows a view using XML with xmln core sap.ui.core.mvc and sap.m. SAP core and m will be discussed in Chapter 2.

It is essential to understand the use of XML in the app when a new view or data connection is needed. This will serve as the primary source navigation from one view to another. For example, we may have a main view, products view and services view to display the content for the application.

```xml
<?xml version="1.0" encoding="UTF-8"?><edmx:Edmx xmlns:edmx="http://schemas.mi
  <edmx:DataServices m:DataServiceVersion="2.0">
    <Schema xmlns="http://schemas.microsoft.com/ado/2008/09/edm" xmlns:sap
      <EntityType Name="DataPoint">
        <Key>
          <PropertyRef Name="TimePoint"/>
        </Key>
        <Property Name="TimePoint" Nullable="false" Type="Edm.DateTime
        <Property Name="Temperature" Type="Edm.Single"/>
        <Property Name="Humidity" Type="Edm.Byte"/>
        <Property Name="DewPoint" Type="Edm.Single"/>
        <Property Name="Pressure" Type="Edm.Int16"/>
        <Property Name="WindSpeed" Type="Edm.Single"/>
        <Property MaxLength="3" Name="WindDirection" Type="Edm.String"
        <Property Name="WindSpeedMax" Type="Edm.Single"/>
        <Property Name="SunRainStart" Type="Edm.Time"/>
        <Property Name="Sun" Type="Edm.Single"/>
        <Property Name="Rain" Type="Edm.Single"/>
        <NavigationProperty FromRole="DataPoint" Name="Note" Relationsl
      </EntityType>
      <EntityType Name="Note">
        <Key>
          <PropertyRef Name="ID"/>
        </Key>
        <Property Name="ID" Nullable="false" Type="Edm.Int32"/>
        <Property Name="StartDate" Nullable="false" Type="Edm.DateTime
        <Property Name="EndDate" Nullable="false" Type="Edm.DateTime"/>
        <Property MaxLength="1024" Name="Details" Nullable="false" Type
        <NavigationProperty FromRole="Note" Name="DataPoints" Relation:
      </EntityType>
      <Association Name="DataPointNote">
```

Figure 1.3: XML data structure

```xml
<mvc:View xmlns:html="http://www.w3.org/1999/xhtml"   xmlns:mvc="sap.ui.core.mvc"
xmlns="sap.m" controllerName="sap.ui.demo.wt.controller.Master">
  <App id="app">
  <Page title="Master view">
  <content>
  <VBox>
  <Label text="Master View" />
  <Button text="Link to next View" press="onPress" />
  </VBox>
  </content>

  </Page>
  </App>
</mvc:View>
```

Figure 1.4: XML view

1.7   Cordova

Apache Cordova is a commonly used protocol when building mobile apps. The framework was first started as PhoneGap and then transitioned to Cordova. Cordova allows developers to build hybrid mobile apps using HTML5, CSS and JavaScript. There are many platforms that work with Cordova so this framework has become extremely popular with both web and mobile developers. The output displays in a web emulator to resemble the mobile device. Table 1.2 outlines some of the popular plugins available to add to the mobile apps. These are common features with mobile apps so many clients and consumers expect these features when operating the apps.

Camera	Capture	Geolocation
Contacts	Accelerometer	Device Information
Network Communication	Battery Status	Compass
Media Playback	Access File	File Transfer
Dialog Notification	Vibration Notification	Globalization
Splash Screen	In-App Browser	Debug Console

Table 1.2: Cordova

Visual Studio, SAP Cloud Platform (Hybrid App Toolkit) and Eclipse support Cordova so developers can use common development environments to build the apps.

1.8   OData

Open Data Protocol (OData) allows for creating, reading, updating and deleting, with data connections. The protocol allows for querying and updating of data with the creation of REST APIs. The features involved include creating, deleting, updating and navigating. However, the data models need to be created to establish the OData connections with the mobile app development environment.

 OData is a standardized model for retrieving data. It is very similar to the concepts of structure query language (SQL). As we know, it is critical for enterprises to access data for daily operations. OData provides a flexible option to connect several data sources, whether the data is online or offline.

OData API

 The OData API provides OData service independence, separation of life cycle, OData querying and consistent API usage, and contains ODataStore API, Payload API and Metadata API (SAP, 2014). The concept of "online" indicates the data is accessed without caching or using local storage on the device.

The example below shows the name space and entity type for the OData Model with Eclipse. As you can see, there is a reference to the services and SAP protocols to retrieve the data.

OData Example

```
<?xml version="1.0" encoding="UTF-8"?><edmx:Edmx
xmlns:edmx="http://schemas.microsoft.com/ado/2007/06/edmx"
xmlns:m="http://schemas.microsoft.com/ado/2007/08/dataservic
es/metadata" Version="1.0">
    <edmx:DataServices m:DataServiceVersion="2.0">
        <Schema
xmlns="http://schemas.microsoft.com/ado/2008/09/edm"
xmlns:sap="http://www.sap.com/Protocols/SAPData"
Namespace="Odatatest">
            <EntityType Name="Entity">
                <Key>
                    <PropertyRef Name="EntityID"/>
                </Key>
                <Property Name="EntityID" Nullable="false"
Type="Edm.String"/>
            </EntityType>
            <EntityContainer Name="default"
m:IsDefaultEntityContainer="true">
                <EntitySet EntityType="Odatatest.Entity"
Name="EntitySet"/>
```

```
        </EntityContainer>
      </Schema>
    </edmx:DataServices>
  </edmx:Edmx>
```

There are several software development lifecycles used to build applications. As with web development, we plan, conduct analysis, design, develop, test, implement and maintain the site. The mobile development lifecycle follows similar principles, but the deployment stage is different since it relies on submission environments such as Apple iOS and Android Play Store for the application to be live in production. As discussed, developers have plenty of options when it comes to developing mobile apps. We will find in coming chapters that you can use Eclipse, SAP Cloud Platform and Visual Studio to build SAPUI5 apps.

2 SAPUI5 Development

SAP has been around since the 1970s, so there is value and demand for building mobile apps with a focus on SAP transactional data. SAPUI5 uses an SAP library and HTML5 for application and mobile application development. SAPUI5 can support XML, JSON and ODATA. You will find in the development that the views are created with XML.

The examples below show the initial index page when creating an HTML5 or SAPUI5 project. The content in this chapter covers each section in more detail, but it is good to compare the structure of an index.html page with just HTML5 code versus an index.html page with SAPUI5. Notice the additional <script> tag, JavaScript variable and CSS needed to develop the project using SAPUI5. Obviously, an HTML5 example would have <script> tags, CSS and JavaScript embedded in the code, but the intent here is to show the basic foundation needed to develop an app with SAPUI5. You can see the similarities with the DOCTYPE, html, head and body.

HTML5 example

```
<!DOCTYPE html>
<html>
<head>
    <meta charset="utf-8" />
    <title></title>
</head>
<body>

</body>
</html>
```

SAPUI5 Example

```
<!DOCTYPE HTML>
<html>
    <head>
        <meta http-equiv="X-UA-Compatible" content="IE=edge">
        <meta http-equiv='Content-Type' content='text/html;charset=UTF-8'/>

        <script src="resources/sap-ui-core.js"
                id="sap-ui-bootstrap"
                data-sap-ui-libs="sap.m"
                data-sap-ui-theme="sap_bluecrystal">
        </script>
        <!-- only load the mobile lib "sap.m" and the "sap_bluecrystal" theme --
>

        <script>
                sap.ui.localResources("starter_app");
                var app = new sap.m.App({initialPage:"idMain1"});
                var page = sap.ui.view({id:"idMain1",
viewName:"starter_app.Main", type:sap.ui.core.mvc.ViewType.XML});
                app.addPage(page);
                app.placeAt("content");
        </script>

    </head>
    <body class="sapUiBody" role="application">
        <div id="content"></div>
    </body>
</html>
```

2.1   Open UI5

SAPUI5 is the focus of app development, but there is also an option to use *OpenUI5*. This is available for everyone, whereas SAPUI5 is available to developers using platforms that support SAP customers. The majority of the controls are available in both environments, with the exception of new editions which are usually featured in the SAPUI5 Development Toolkit for HTML5 (see Chapter 10).

OpenUI5

This is an open source JavaScript library for building enterprise applications. The open source environment provides a software development kit (SDK) for development needs.

SAPUI5 is very flexible because it can be used with *Eclipse, SAP Cloud Platform* and *Visual Studio,* along with many other development options. Table 2.1 lists the libraries supported for SAPUI5. The sap.m library is used in this book because it contains the necessary controls for mobile app development. Mobile apps also use sap.ui for user experience and standard controls.

sap.ui.comp	sap.m	sap.table
sap.ca	sap.me	sap.ushell
sap.uxap	sap.gantt	sap.ui.core
sap.ui.layout	sap.ui.unified	sap.ui.table
sap.viz		

Table 2.1: SAPUI5 libraries

The namespace sap.m is used for mobile devices and desktops. A list of all available controls is located under the API Reference tab in the SAPUI5 Development Toolkit.

2.2   SAPUI5 Development Toolkit

SAPUI5 offers a dynamic demo kit for SAP developers. Developers have the option to view code and examples for *Action, Chart, Container, Data Binding, Display, Layout, List, Map, Popup, Routing, Testing, Theme* or *Tile* using the SAPUI5 Development Toolkit. Samples of code snippets or solutions can be accessed through the SAPUI5 Development Toolkit. The Development Toolkit helps developers test examples and then use the code for their mobile app development. SAP's willingness to provide this demo kit increases the use and acceptance of the SAPUI5 framework. Table 2.2 outlines the tab options available with the SAPUI5 Development Toolkit.

Tab	Description
DEVELOPER GUIDE	Provides a list of supports such as Tutorials, Essentials, Developing Apps Documentation and Templates
EXPLORED	Offers control examples outlining properties, events and methods
API REFERENCE	Provides a list of controls with the namespace sap.ui, sap.m, sap.chart, sap.m.routing, along with many others
DEMO APPS	Provides over twelve sample apps that can be explored, with the option to download the source code to import into the development environment
ICONS	Offers options for common icons used in the SAPUI5 apps
CONTROLS	Provides a gallery of simple to advanced controls

Table 2.2: SAPUI5 Development Toolkit

As you can see, there are plenty of learning opportunities and code examples to build apps. This can sometimes be an issue when considering a new mobile development environment – for instance, there is an abundance of mobile development options, but few offer code examples, demonstrations, templates and libraries to this degree.

2.3   ListBox

List boxes and items allow us to organize content as sections to be displayed on the page. As seen in the example below, the SAPUI5 Development Toolkit provides the structure and example of the ListBox code. It is important to note that this is only the JavaScript, which can be nested in the index.html page or listed as a function in the controller.js page. We will discuss the controllers more in the Model View Controller (MVC) section.

Exercise – ListBox review

1. Open the *SAP Demo Kit* (see Chapter 10)
2. Click on the CONTROLS tab
3. Click on the VALUEHOLDERS section, expand the selection
4. Click on LISTBOX
5. View the sample code snippets under the Examples section

The example of the ListBox below shows the items, function for the text summary and multi selection checkbox. We will not use this specific ListBox in any tutorials, but it is good know that this code snippet is available for future needs.

ListBox example

```
// Create the ListBox
var oSimpleListBox = new sap.ui.commons.ListBox({
    items: [
        new sap.ui.core.ListItem({ text: 'Spring' }),
        new sap.ui.core.ListItem({ text: 'Summer' }),
        new sap.ui.core.ListItem({ text: 'Autumn' }),
        new sap.ui.core.ListItem({ text: 'Winter' })
    ],
    select: function (e) {
        var a = ["Your favorite season(s): "];
        jQuery.each(oSimpleListBox.getSelectedItems(),
function (idx, item) { a.push(item.getText(), ","); });
        oTextSummary.setText(a.join(""));
    }
}).placeAt("sample1");
var oTextSummary = new
sap.ui.commons.TextView().placeAt("sample1");
var oMultiSelectionCheckBox = new sap.ui.commons.CheckBox({
    text: "MultiSelection",
    checked: false,
```

```
    change: function (e) {
oSimpleListBox.setAllowMultiSelect(e.getSource().getChecked(
)); }
}).placeAt("sample1");
```

Let's now take a look at another control source code. Buttons are commonly used with mobile apps for navigation or to perform a particular event.

Exercise – Button review

1. In the SAPUI5 DEVELOPMENT TOOLKIT, click on the CONTROLS tab

2. Type Button in the search box

3. Click on BUTTON under SIMPLECONTROLS

4. Scroll down to the EXAMPLES to review the code snippets

The example below shows the sample code when making the selections in the exercise above. Note the variable with the oButton1, function alert and placeAt location. We will use this sample code for the button when working with Visual Studio in Chapter 10.

Button code example

```
// create a simple button with some text and a tooltip only
var oButton1 = new sap.ui.commons.Button({
    text: "Button",
    tooltip: "This is a test tooltip",
    press: function () { alert('Alert from ' +
oButton1.getText()); }
});
// attach it to some element in the page
oButton1.placeAt("sample1");
```

As mentioned before, the use of the SAPUI5 Development Toolkit can serve as a guide for developing mobile apps. It is recommended to review the controls and demo apps in order to understand the structure and available controls.

2.4   SAPUI5 libraries

The types of SAPUI5 libraries include commons, mobile, visualizations, user interface and tables, along with others. The libraries are in the application layer to be presented on mobile devices or desktops. We can control the libraries with XML, JavaScript and HTML pages. Luckily, we can use device detection to determine and adjust the app depending on the viewing device.

SAPUI5 has many namespaces to be used for development. Table 2.3 shows a limited list of namespaces and classes. Please note this is only a preview. All namespaces and classes can be found under the API REFERENCE tab in the SAPUI5 Development Toolkit.

Namespace	Classes
sap.m	Mobile ActionListItem, Bar, Button, Carousel, CheckBox, ComboBox, Dialog, List, Menu, NavContainer, TextArea, Table, VBox
sap.viz.ui5	Dataset, ChartFormatter,
sap.ui.commons	Text fields, buttons, message boxes and scrolls
sap.ui.table	Library for chart controls

Table 2.3: SAPUI5 libraries

This book will focus on using sap.m. In Figure 2.1, the sap.m library is used inside the scripts of the index.html file. The sap.m library is a namespace that includes controls such as *App*, *Button*, *Carousel*, *CheckBox*, *ComboBox*, *NavContainer*, *RadioButton* and *VBox*, to name but a few.

sap.m control tip

 An updated list of *sap.m controls* can be found in the API REFERENCE tab in the SAPUI5 DEVELOPMENT TOOLKIT.

In Figure 2.1, the index.html page displays the <script> tags, which have the SAP namespaces and libraries.

```
<script id="sap-ui-bootstrap"
    src="../../resources/sap-ui-core.js"
    data-sap-ui-libs="sap.m"
    data-sap-ui-theme="sap_bluecrystal"
    data-sap-ui-compatVersion="edge"
    data-sap-ui-resourceroots='{"sapui5LastName": ""}'>
</script>

<link rel="stylesheet" type="text/css" href="css/style.css">

<script>
    sap.ui.getCore().attachInit(function() {
        new sap.m.Shell({
            app: new sap.ui.core.ComponentContainer({
                height : "100%",
                name : "sapui5LastName"
            })
        }).placeAt("content");
    });
</script>
</head>
```

Figure 2.1: SAPUI5 libraries

Note the *new sap.m.Shell* and *new sap.ui.core* statements within the <script> tag. Let's now review a few additional sap.m controls. Table 2.4 shows some *sap.m controls* that we will use in later exercises in this book.

sap.m Control	Code Description
sap.m.Button	new sap.m.Button(sId?, mSettings?)
sap.m.List	new sap.m.List(sId?, mSettings?)
sap.m.TextArea	sap.m.TextArea(sId?, mSettings?)
sap.m.MessageBox	sap.m.MessageBox
sap.m.VBox	new sap.m.VBox(sId?, mSettings?)

Table 2.4: sap.m controls

Let's take a look at the *TextArea* control. The SAPUI5 demo kit provides many code examples for the controls. In the SAPUI5 TextArea control example, the code uses the new sap.ui.commons to create the TextArea. However, we are building a mobile app so we need to adjust the code to new sap.m.TextArea, as seen in the modified TextArea control example.

TextArea control example

```
oInput = new sap.ui.commons.TextArea('input1');
oInput.setValue("Here is some Text. I hope you like it.");
oInput.setTooltip("This is a tooltip");
oInput.setRows(3);
oInput.attachChange(function () { alert('Text changed to :'
+ oInput.getValue()); });

// attach it to some element in the page
oInput.placeAt("content");
```

We can add the *sap.m controls* with the *new sap.m.* The mobile control will be substituted with the particular control needed. Note the difference between the *sap.ui.commons* and *sap.m TextArea control* in both examples.

sap.m TextArea control example

```
oInput = new sap.m.TextArea('input1');
oInput.setValue("Here is some text");
oInput.setTooltip("This is a tooltip");
oInput.setRows(3);
oInput.attachChange(function () { alert('Text changed to:' +
oInput.getValue()); });

//attach it to some element in the page
oInput.placeAt("content");
```

2.5 Themes

The style of an app is very important for the overall theme. Styling is performed with the use of CSS. This CSS is associated with the desired theme. Table 2.5 shows the available themes that can be incorporated into SAPUI5 apps.

Base	sap_bluecrystal
sap_hcb	sap_goldreflection
sap_ux	
sap_platinum	

Table 2.5: Themes

In the Blue Crystal theme example below, the sap-ui-core.js file loads the SAP Framework while the app uses the *Blue Crystal theme*. Figure 2.2 provides a display of a Blue Crystal theme while Figure 2.3 shows a *Gold Reflection theme*. It is relatively easy to make the adjustment by changing the code inside the script tag.

Blue Crystal theme example

```
<script src="resources/sap-ui-core.js"
    id="sap-ui-bootstrap"
    data-sap-ui-libs="sap.m"
    data-sap-ui-theme="sap_bluecrystal">
</script>
```

Gold Reflection theme example

```
<script src="resources/sap-ui-core.js"
    id="sap-ui-bootstrap"
    data-sap-ui-libs="sap.m"
    data-sap-ui-theme="sap_goldreflection">
</script>
```

Figure 2.2: Blue Crystal theme

Figure 2.3: Gold Reflection theme

In this chapter, we have covered the basics for using SAPUI5 along with the sap.m library and available controls. Remember, the SAPUI5 Development Toolkit is a necessity when building apps because it acts as a great reference and provides code snippets to speed up development.

3 Model View Controller (MVC)

Many development platforms use Model View Controller (MVC) for applications, mobile development and web development. This is an effective development framework with the use of HTML5, JavaScript, CSS, Views, Models and Controllers. As mentioned previously, SAPUI5 can utilize MVC.

Let's examine each component of the MVC framework. The model is responsible for managing the data used with the mobile app. There are several models that can be used for data integration into apps. Examples of these models include *JSON*, *XML*, *OData* and *Resource*. Table 3.1 shows available models and descriptions.

Model	Description
JSON Model	Binds controls to JavaScript on client
XML Model	Binds node structure with character strings on client
OData Model	Binds to a database model as an extract from the database or load from server
Resource Model	Used for binding with static text

Table 3.1: Models

It is important to understand that you can use one or a combination of these models to build a mobile app.

Views are used to display the content with the user interface. These are the pages that the users will interact with. There are several types of views that can be created such as *XML*, *JSON*, *JavaScript* and *HTML*. Usually, the `<div id='content'>` tag will be associated with the first view. The views associated in the index page will populate information, controls and content using the desired view structure. For example, you will use a `Main.view.xml` for *XML views* and `Main.view.js` for *JavaScript views*. Figure 3.1 shows the file structures for both an *SAPUI5 XML View* and *SAPUI5 JavaScript View Development Paradigm*.

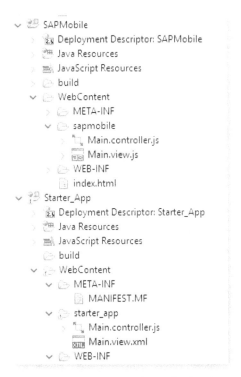

Figure 3.1: XML view and JavaScript view

The controller manages the control of data and events for the views and model. We can add events in the controllers to populate in the views. Table 3.2 provides the hooks that can be called in the controller.js pages.

Hooks	Description
onInt()	Called when view controller is instantiated onInit: function() {},
onExit	Invoked when control is closed onExit: function() {}
onAfterRendering()	Invoked when View is rendered onAfterRendering: function() {},
onBeforeRendering()	Invoked before View is rendered onBeforeRendering: function() {},

Table 3.2: Controller

A key feature with this development approach is the ability to reuse and connect code with multiple pages or views. In Figure 3.2, note the interaction between the view, model and controller. This is important so that the code can be segmented instead of placing all content, data connections, events and controls in one file.

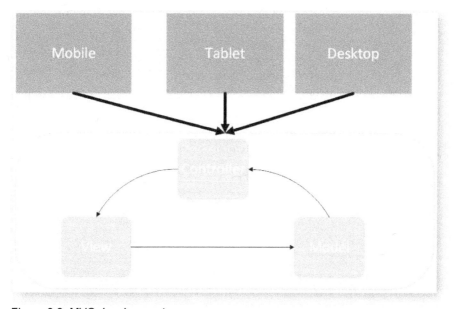

Figure 3.2: MVC development

The following code examples show the creation of an SAPUI5 MVC project. The `index.html`, `View.view.xml` and `View.controller.js` are created with this MVC development framework. An *html file*, *xml view* and *controller* are needed to make the MVC framework work. The model can be created once the data approach (i.e. OData, JSON or XML) is selected for the app.

3.1 HTML Example

The *index page* is the initial page where we identify the theme, libraries, resources, views and type of MVC (i.e. XML, JSON, HTML or JavaScript) approach. The example below shows an initial html page outlining the content needed for the MVC application. SAP names and libraries were already discussed in Chapter 2, but we now want to focus on the contents in the script tag for this page.

Index.html example

```html
<!DOCTYPE HTML>
<html>
  <head>
    <meta http-equiv="X-UA-Compatible" content="IE=edge">
    <meta http-equiv='Content-Type'
content='text/html;charset=UTF-8'/>

    <script src="resources/sap-ui-core.js"
        id="sap-ui-bootstrap"
        data-sap-ui-libs="sap.m"
        data-sap-ui-theme="sap_bluecrystal">
    </script>
    <!-- only load the mobile lib "sap.m" and the
"sap_bluecrystal" theme -->

    <script>
        sap.ui.localResources("sapui5_xml_view");
        var app = new sap.m.App({initialPage:"idView1"});
        var page = sap.ui.view({id:"idView1",
viewName:"sapui5_xml_view.View",
type:sap.ui.core.mvc.ViewType.XML});
        app.addPage(page);
        app.placeAt("content");
    </script>

  </head>
  <body class="sapUiBody" role="application">
    <div id="content"></div>
  </body>
</html>
```

Table 3.3 describes the contents in the <script> tag and the description notes for each.

Script Tag Contents	Description
`src="resources/sap-ui-core.js"`	Local resources
`var app = new sap.m.App({initialPage:"idView1"});`	New app
`var page = sap.ui.view({id:"idView1", viewName:"sapui5_xml_view.View", type:sap.ui.core.mvc.ViewType.XML});`	Id of initial view
`app.addPage(page);`	Add view to `index.html` **page**
`app.placeAt("content");`	Place view contents to `<div id="content"> </div>` in the `<body>` tag

Table 3.3: Script contents

In Table 3.3, note the `app.PlaceAt("content")`. This code instructs the `index.html` page to place the content from the `View.view.xml` page in the `<div>` tag. The body tag example below shows the `id="content"` within the body class.

Body tag example

```
<body class="sapUiBody" role="application">
    <div id="content"></div>
</body>
```

3.2   View example

Views are located in the View folder within the Web Content or Web App Structure.

View folder

 It may be necessary to create a View folder within the Web Content folder if it does not already exist. This may be the case when developing in Eclipse or Visual Studio.

In the example below, note the structure of the controllerName xml_view.View. If you recall, this was also listed in Table 3.3 of the index.html page. This is the view that will populate the initial view of the app since the information within the <content> tag will show within the <div id="content"></div> of the index.html page.

View example

```
<core:View xmlns:core="sap.ui.core"
xmlns:mvc="sap.ui.core.mvc" xmlns="sap.m"
    controllerName="sapui5_xml_view.View"
xmlns:html="http://www.w3.org/1999/xhtml">
  <Page title="Title">
    <content>

    </content>
  </Page>
</core:View>
```

Let's take a look at an example using JavaScript for the view. We will use JavaScript for the view with Eclipse development. Figure 3.3 shows the location of the JavaScript file along with the Script code nested inside the View.js file.

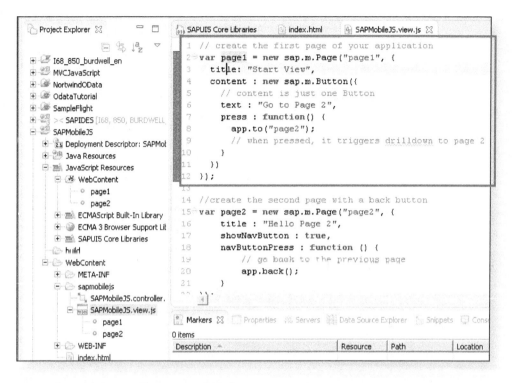

Figure 3.3: JavaScript view of MVC

3.3   Model example

The model of the framework manages the application data. Earlier in the chapter we discussed the different types of mobile use. They are OData, JSON, XML and Resource models. Figure 3.4 provides an example of a JavaScript model.

```
models.js  ×
1 ▾ sap.ui.define([
2        "sap/ui/model/json/JSONModel",
3        "sap/ui/Device"
4 ▾ ], function(JSONModel, Device) {
5        "use strict";
6
7 ▾    return {
8
9 ▾        createDeviceModel: function() {
10               var oModel = new JSONModel(Device);
11               oModel.setDefaultBindingMode("OneWay");
12               return oModel;
13           }
14
15        };
16  });
```

Figure 3.4: Model example

Overall, we want to see how everything looks with the MVC model. Figure 3.5 shows the entire file structure with the index.html, xml, controller and model.

- ListView
  - webapp
    - controller
      - Detail.controller.js
      - View1.controller.js
    - css
    - i18n
    - model
      - models.js
    - view
      - Detail.view.xml
      - View1.view.xml
    - Component.js
    - index.html
    - manifest.json
  - .project.json
  - neo-app.json

Figure 3.5: MVC file structure

3.4 Controller example

The next step is to review the controller. Remember, a controller is created once a view is established. Controllers will relate to a particular view. As mentioned above, the hooks for the controller are onInit:function(), onBeforeRendering:function(), onAfter Rendering:function() and onExit:function(). Figure 3.6 shows a common association with the *View1* and *Detail views* correlated with the *View1* and *Detail controllers*. The examples of the View1.xml and controller are listed below the figure.

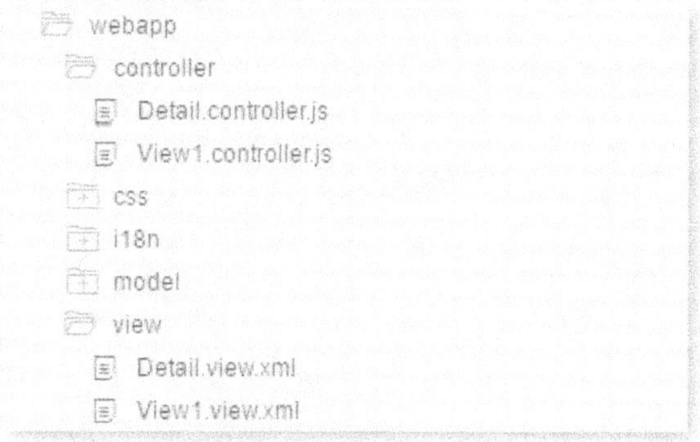

Figure 3.6: Views and controllers

View1.view.xml example

```
<mvc:View
controllerName="HelloWorldHelloWorld.controller.View1"
xmlns:html="http://www.w3.org/1999/xhtml"
xmlns:mvc="sap.ui.core.mvc"
        displayBlock="true" xmlns="sap.m">
  <App>
    <pages>
      <Page title="{i18n>title}">
        <content>
          <List items="{/Products}">
            <StandardListItem type="Navigation"
press="handleListItemPress" title="{ProductName}"/>
          </List>
        </content>
      </Page>
```

```
        </pages>
      </App>
  </mvc:View>
```

View1.controller.js example

```
sap.ui.define([
    "sap/ui/core/mvc/Controller"
], function (Controller) {
    "use strict";

    return Controller.extend("HelloWorld.controller.View1",
{
        handleListItemPress: function (evt) {
            var oRouter =
sap.ui.core.UIComponent.getRouterFor(this);
            var selectedProductId =
evt.getSource().getBindingContext().getProperty("ProductID")
;
            oRouter.navTo("detail", {
                productId: selectedProductId
            });
        }

    });

});
```

As we have discovered, MVC can be instrumental in mobile develop-ment. This approach allows the developer to position code in an HTML page, view, controller and model. This helps with clarity and efficiency in developing apps.

4 SAPUI5 apps with Eclipse

For over 20 years, developers have been creating applications with Eclipse. There have been millions of downloads with this environment so it is extremely popular. Luckily, Eclipse supports SAPUI5 with the UI Development Toolkit so developers have the opportunity to create mobile apps using Eclipse with the structure of SAPUI5. This is extremely beneficial because Eclipse users can work with a familiar platform within the SAPUI5 framework.

4.1 Install Eclipse Java Development Kit (JDK)

Developers can develop mobile apps with SAPUI5 within the *Eclipse Java Development KIT (JDK) environment.* An advantage of using the JDK is the ability to build SAPUI5 apps using the UI Development package and to connect to a database using the SAP Mobile Platform package.

The first step to building an SAPUI5 app with Eclipse is to download the environment.

Exercise – Eclipse download

1. Go to the following page:
   http://www.eclipse.org/downloads/
2. Download the latest Eclipse package
3. Install the executable file

Figure 4.1 shows the option you need to select once you run the executable file. Note that you may need to download supporting Java files before the application will install. This environment can develop apps with Java, but the focus of this context is to extend the platform to SAPUI5.

Eclipse IDE for Java Developers

The essential tools for any Java developer, including a Java IDE, a Git client, XML Editor, Mylyn, Maven and Gradle integration

Figure 4.1: Eclipse IDE for Java developers

The environment will be available to you once the install has been successful. Note in Figure 4.2 the project structure and run button. We will use both the panel and run command many times in this chapter.

Figure 4.2: Eclipse environment

4.2   SAP development tools

The next step of the process is to install the necessary tools to develop the SAPUI5 apps in Eclipse. You first have to install new software before creating an SAPUI5 app. The SAP development tools need to be added once Eclipse has been successfully installed on the machine.

Exercise – Development tools

1. Click on HELP in Eclipse
2. Select INSTALL NEW SOFTWARE
3. Enter https://tools.hana.ondemand.com/neon in the WORK WITH textbox
4. For this example, we will select the UI DEVELOPMENT TOOLKIT FOR HTML5 (see Figure 4.3)
5. Click NEXT, NEXT, Select TERMS, Click FINISH

Figure 4.3 shows the available software for the current version of Eclipse. The UI Development Toolkit for HTML5 is the option used for this exercise, but there are other options available such as Cloud Platform Tools, SAP HANA Tools and SAP Identity Management Tools.

Name

> ☐ 000 ABAP Development Tools for SAP NetWeaver
> ☐ 000 Modeling Tools for SAP BW powered by SAP HANA
> ☐ 000 SAP Cloud Platform Tools
> ☐ 000 SAP HANA Tools
> ☐ 000 SAP Identity Management Tools
> ☑ 000 UI Development Toolkit for HTML5

Figure 4.3: Eclipse available software

Use the right Eclipse version

Please be aware of the Eclipse version you are working with. At the time of writing this content, Eclipse Neon does not provide the SAP Mobile Platform tools which are needed for the SAP Mobile Platform Server. However, Eclipse Luna does provide these tools with on-demand download. The SAP Mobile Platform tool will be used in Chapter 5.

Now that the development toolkit has been added we are ready to create our first app with SAPUI5.

Exercise – SMP mobile test app

1. In Eclipse, Select FILE, NEW

2. Select SAPUI5 APPLICATION DEVELOPMENT; APPLICATION PROJECT

3. NEXT

4. PROJECT NAME: SAPMobile {the application name can only contain the following: Latin characters, minus symbols, dots or underscore}. Note the *sap.m* for the Library

5. NEXT

6. Leave the Folder as the default

7. NAME: Main {This is for the view, leave default as JavaScript},

8. NEXT

9. Select YES to open the perspective

Figure 4.4 provides the dialog box of the *Project name*, *Library* and *Options* during the application creation process.

Once the new app is created we need to examine the index.html page. The index page provides sap-ui-core.js, sap-ui-boostrap, sap.m and sap.bluecrystal in the <script> tag, as shown in Figure 4.5. These concepts were covered in Chapter 2, where the use of SAPUI5 was explained.

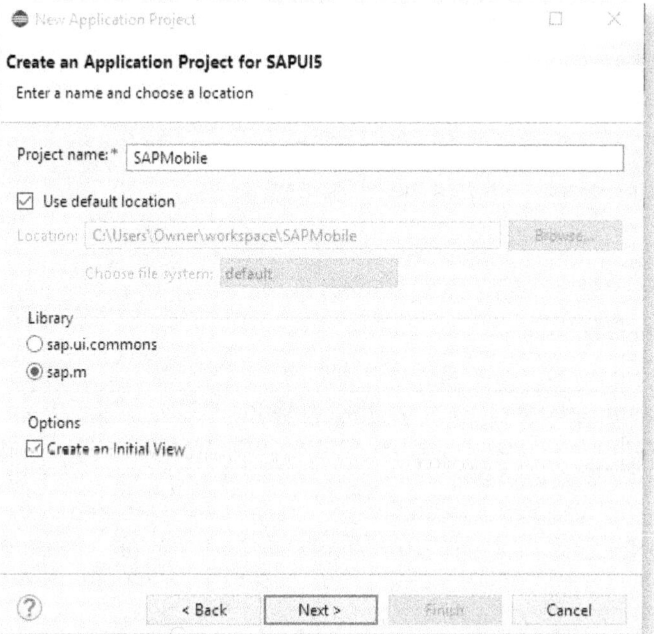

Figure 4.4: SAPUI5 new app

```
1  <!DOCTYPE HTML>
2  <html>
3      <head>
4          <meta http-equiv="X-UA-Compatible" content="IE=edge">
5          <meta http-equiv='Content-Type' content='text/html;charset=UTF-8'/>
6
7          <script src="resources/sap-ui-core.js"
8              id="sap-ui-bootstrap"
9              data-sap-ui-libs="sap.m"
10             data-sap-ui-theme="sap_bluecrystal">
11         </script>
12         <!-- only load the mobile lib "sap.m" and the "sap_bluecrystal" theme -
13
14         <script>
15             sap.ui.localResources("sapmobile");
16             var app = new sap.m.App({initialPage:"idMain1"});
17             var page = sap.ui.view({id:"idMain1", viewName:"sapmobile.Main"
18             app.addPage(page);
19             app.placeAt("content");
20         </script>
21
22     </head>
23     <body class="sapUiBody" role="application">
24         <div id="content"></div>
25     </body>
26 </html>
```

Figure 4.5: SAPUI5 index page

It is now time to run the app for the first preview.

Exercise – Preview

1. Open the `index.html` page
2. Select RUN from the MENU BAR,
3. Click RUN
4. Select WEB APP PREVIEW
5. Click OK

This is an excellent opportunity to instantly view the SAPUI5 app. Some mobile app development environments require the developer to download additional SDKs or to install a device to preview the app. There are certainly benefits to downloading additional emulators, SDKs and devices, but this can be very time intensive. Figure 4.6 shows the output for the first app. As you will notice, it is not simulated in a mobile device emulator, but can be a very useful tool when testing the code.

Java EE - Eclipse
File Edit Navigate Search Project Run Window Help

Project Explorer
MVC
SMP_Mobile_Test

index.html   index.html
http://localhost:11600/SMP_Mobile_Test/index.html

Markers   Properties   Servers   Snippets

Figure 4.6: SAP UI5 app using Eclipse Luna

4.3 Push button and text app

Now that we have this working, let's go back to the SAP Demo Kit covered in Chapter 2. We want to examine the use of a button and text controls. If we click on the API REFERENCE TAB in the SAP Development Toolkit (see Chapter 10), we can review the features of a button and text by simply typing in sap.m.button or sap.m.text. The following tips show the descriptions, properties and events associated with a mobile button and text. This is a good indication of what you can do with each control as well as with the events that can be applied to it.

4.3.1 sap.m.Button

A button control can provide a *save*, *print*, *navigation* or *action command*.

Properties

- ▶ text
- ▶ type
- ▶ width
- ▶ enabled
- ▶ icon
- ▶ iconFirst
- ▶ activeIcon
- ▶ iconDensityAware
- ▶ textDirection

Events

- ▶ tap
- ▶ press

4.3.2   sap.m.Text

Used for embedding text paragraphs.

Properties

- ▶ text
- ▶ textDirection
- ▶ wrapping
- ▶ textAlign
- ▶ width
- ▶ maxLines

In the exercises for Eclipse, we will focus on using JavaScript for the initial view. When developing apps in the SAP Cloud Platform and Visual Studio we will focus on using XML views. Let's create another app using the *sap.m library* with a button and text.

Exercise – Button and text app

1. In Eclipse, select FILE, NEW, OTHER

2. **SAPUI5 Application Development, Application Project**

3. NEXT

4. PROJECT NAME: button_text_app

5. **Ensure sap.m is selected** under LIBRARY (see Figure 4.7)

6. NEXT

7. NAME: Main

8. DEVELOPMENT PARADIGM: JAVASCRIPT (see Figure 4.8)

9. FINISH

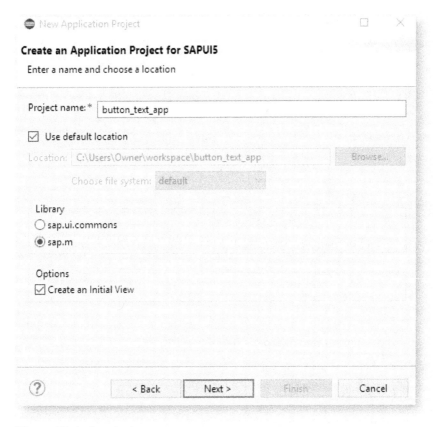

Figure 4.7: button_text_app

51

Figure 4.8: Create new view

Let's now try to add a button with an action, along with a text control.

Exercise – Review code examples

1. Open the `index.html` page
2. Review the code examples
3. Notice the `id=content` inside of the `<body>` tag. This was discussed earlier in Chapter 3.

index.html body example

```
<body class="sapUiBody" role="application">
  <div id="content"></div>
</body>
```

The id content is located in the *createContent* in the `Main.view.js` file.

Main.view.js createContent example

```
createContent : function(oController) {
    return new sap.m.Page({
      title: "Title",
      content: [

      ]
    });
}
```

We can add controls to the *oController* to be displayed in the `index.html` page. Below we will modify the createContent to include the *oController* in the `Main.view.js`.

Modify the `createContent` **section**

You only want to modify the `createContent` section. Do not adjust the `sap.ui.jsview` or `getControllerName` function.

Exercise – Modify the `createContent` **code**

1. In the `Main.view.js` file:

2. Modify the `createContent` code with the example below

Main.view.js oController example

```
createContent : function(oController) {
    return new sap.m.Page({
      title: "Button and Text",
      content: [

        new sap.m.Button({
          text: "press button",
          press: function(){
              alert("Welcome Button and Text")
          }
          }),

        new sap.m.Text({text: "Hello Button and Text"})

      ]
    })
  }
```

Now let's run the app.

Exercise – Run as Web App Preview

1. Select the `index.html` page
2. Select RUN, RUN AS, WEB APP PREVIEW
3. Click the PRESS button to view the ALERT MESSAGE
4. Note the message from the function (see Figure 4.9)

This exercise was established to show how to create a JavaScript using an event to display a message. We will now move into the integration of Eclipse with the SAP Mobile Platform Server and SAP Mobile SDK.

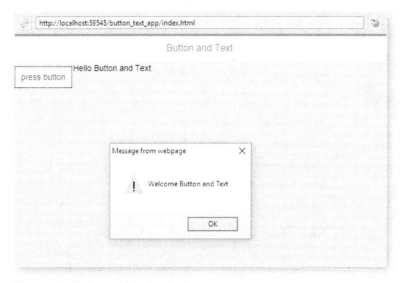

Figure 4.9: Button and text output

4.4   SAP Development tools for Eclipse

We can use SAP Development tools to connect to an SMP Server and OData using Eclipse. However, we have to install these tools.

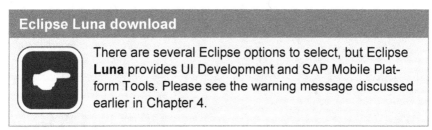

Eclipse Luna download

There are several Eclipse options to select, but Eclipse **Luna** provides UI Development and SAP Mobile Platform Tools. Please see the warning message discussed earlier in Chapter 4.

If you are using Eclipse Luna, you can add the *SAP Mobile Platform Tools* to the environment. This will provide additional connection opportunities to the SAP Mobile Platform Server.

Exercise – SAP Mobile Platform Tools install

1. In Eclipse Luna, click on HELP

2. Select INSTALL NEW SOFTWARE

3. Enter https://tools.hana.ondemand.com/luna in the WORK WITH textbox

4. Click ADD

5. Check the SAP MOBILE PLATFORM TOOLS CHECKBOX (see Figure 4.10)

6. Click NEXT

7. Click FINISH

Available Software

Check the items that you wish to install.

Work with: SAP Development Tools for Eclipse Luna - https://tools.hana.ondemand.com/luna   Add...

Find more software by working with the "Available Software Sites" preferences.

type filter text

Name	Version
ABAP Development Tools for SAP NetWeaver	
Modeling Tools for SAP BW powered by SAP HANA	
SAP HANA Cloud Integration Tools (Deprecated)	
SAP HANA Cloud Platform Tools	
SAP HANA Tools	
SAP Identity Management Tools	
SAP Mobile Platform Tools	
UI Development Toolkit for HTML5	

Select All   Deselect All

Details

☑ Show only the latest versions of available software   ☑ Hide items that are already installed

☑ Group items by category   What is already installed?

☐ Show only software applicable to target environment

☑ Contact all update sites during install to find required software

?   < Back   Next >   Finish   Cancel

Figure 4.10: Eclipse Luna tools

You will not notice much at this point, but we need to perform this task in order to make the connection to the SAP mobile platform server. We will now cover the usefulness and purpose of using the SAP Mobile Platform.

4.5 Create OData web service

Another feature included with the SAP Mobile Server Toolkit is *OData services*. The SMP with Eclipse allows developers to connect to *SQL Anywhere, SQL Server, Oracle, IBM DB2, Simple Object Access Protocol* (SOAP) and *SAP NetWeaver Gateway*. Figure 4.11 shows the data flow from an e-commerce site from the SMP Server. OData is a standardized model for retrieving data. It is very similar to the concepts of structure query language (SQL). It provides another option for enterprises to access data for employee operations. OData offers a flexible option to connect several data sources whether the data is online or offline.

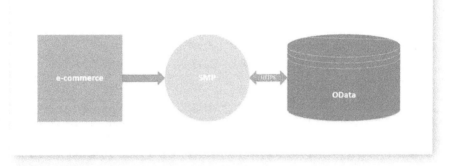

Figure 4.11: SMP Odata

OData API	
	The OData API provides OData service independence, separation of life cycle, OData querying and consistent API usage, and contains ODataStore API, Payload API and Metadata API (SAP, 2014)[1].The concept of "online" indicates the data is accessed without caching or using local storage on the device.

We can now create a project using OData.

---

[1] SAP (2014). Native OData App Development Using the OData API.

Exercise – OData

1. In Eclipse: Select FILE, NEW, OTHER
2. SAP MOBILE PLATFORM
3. SAP MOBILE PLATFORM ODATA IMPLEMENTATION PROJECT
4. Enter Weather as the PROJECT NAME (see Figure 4.12)
5. Click NEXT
6. Enter Weather as MODEL NAME (see Figure 4.13)
7. Click NEXT
8. Enter Web Service URL (see Figure 4.14)
9. Click GO
10. Note the SERVICE DETAILS (see Figure 4.14)
11. Click FINISH
12. Review the ODATA DIAGRAM (see Figure 4.15)

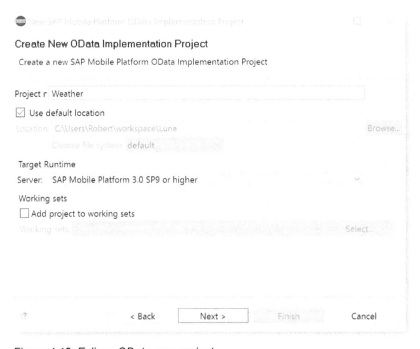

Figure 4.12: Eclipse OData new project

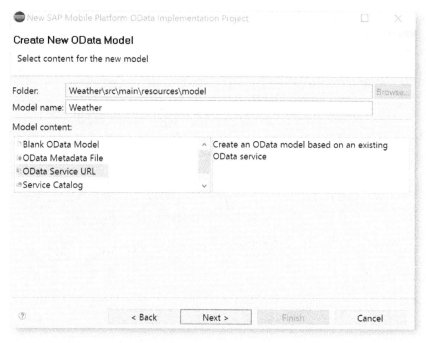

Figure 4.13: Eclipse OData model name

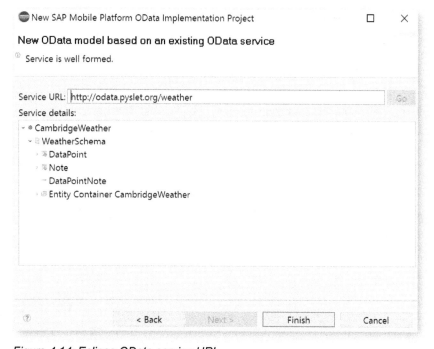

Figure 4.14: Eclipse OData service URL

The web service appears as a new project with schema and relationships. Find the Weather.odata file to review the entities and properties.

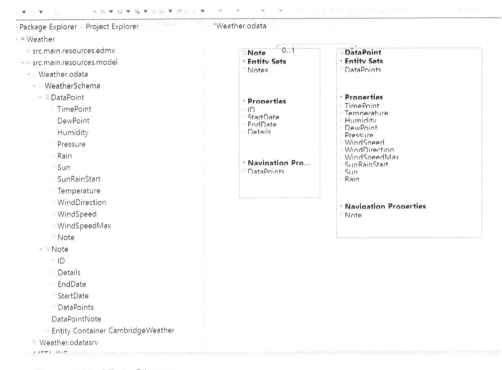

Figure 4.15: OData Diagram

This OData connection process allows you to retrieve data from online or off-line data sources to integrate into mobile apps. The benefit of using a process like this is that the data is located in the same environment and file structure as the mobile app development.

5 SAP Mobile Platform Server

The SMP Server provides administration and monitoring options for monitoring tasks, applications, clusters, settings, reporting and logs. Additionally, there are services available such as application analytics, HTTP(s) configuration, application resources, data integration, management cockpit and security support.

The SMP Server platform is used to deploy, manage and monitor mobile apps, to manage connections, users and applications, and to review usage, logs and profiles. A major advantage to building an SAPUI5 app with Eclipse is the ability to connect to the SAP Mobile Platform Server and utilize the SAP Mobile SDK. This provides the opportunity to develop the apps in Eclipse and then deploy to the SAP mobile platform server, as well as to utilize the SAP Gateway.

SAP Mobile consists of two major components: *SMP Server* and *SDK* (software development kit). The SMP Server offers access to administration and monitoring, integration gateway and data integration while the SDK provides options for development using different environments. It is recommended to review the SMP Server and SDK documentation prior to installation in order to understand the operating and environment requirements.

SMP Server includes an Open Service Gateway Initiative (OSGi) for classes and configurations that work with core and application services. Table 5.1 displays the core services and application services available within the OSGi container.

Application Analytics	App Resources	Data Integration
HTTP(s) Configuration	Life Cycle Management	Management Cockpit
Persistence	Push Notifications	Security Profile
Agentry Data Services	Offline OData Services	Supportability

Table 5.1: SMP OSGi container

Application analytics shows the options for usage statistics, registrations, requests, response times and details regarding the applications. Additionally, data integration provides connections between SAP and non-SAP databases. SMP allows for multiple database connections such as HANA, SQL Anywhere, SQL Server and Oracle database. There are plugin options in the development platforms to make OData connections.

SMP and SDK documentation

SMP installation documentation provides links for the SAP Help Portal and installation guide for Windows or Linux. There are several installation guides for Windows and Linux. Please see the SMP link in Chapter 10.

The previous version (SMP 2.0) only allowed for development with an unwired server and mobile platform. Developers created the data connection, developed the mobile business object, and then deployed as a hybrid app. This approach was suitable, but it limited developers to a single platform for building mobile apps. Additionally, there was no console for developers to manage the mobile apps.

An advancement of SMP 3.0 over SMP 2.0 is the ability to select a preferred environment for development. There are a range of SDKs available with the SMP SDK installation. This strategy also supports Bring Your Own Tools (BYOT) to develop mobile apps within the environment.

Figure 5.1 illustrates how the Sap Mobile Platform 3.0 (SMP) interacts with the SDKs for development and data backend services. It is important to see how a developer can use a variety of tools and databases to connect with the SMP Server. The communication between the SDK and SMP is done using HTTPS while the backend may have different connection protocols depending on the specific database or service used. In this instance, we are developing apps with SAPUI5 using Eclipse so the development is considered hybrid.

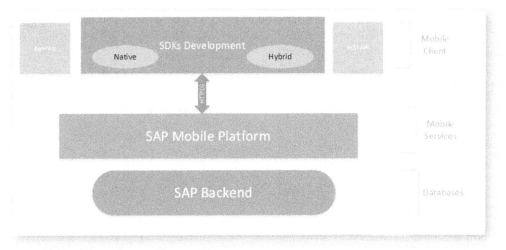

Figure 5.1: SAP Mobile Platform

The mobile client includes the *Agentry Container, Customer App, Kapsel* and *Browser previews* as seen in Figure 5.2 for mobile testing. This is an impressive feature given the client's ability to develop mobile apps with several environments. Again, this gives developers the option to create mobile apps with SAP UI5, CSS and JavaScript using an MVC approach.

Agentry	Custom App	Kapsel
Browsers	SDKs	UI5

Table 5.2: Mobile client

5.1 SMP server purchase options

The initial step in connecting a mobile app with SMP is to determine the purchase options for development. It is best to review all options to ensure the selection is appropriate for both short-term and long-term development needs.

63

The SMP provides a trial environment using a cloud service or options to purchase SMP 3.0 depending on the use. Table 5.3 shows the available purchase options for SMP.

Purchase options	Description
Single app option	Create one app
Full use	Create multiple applications with one user
Developer edition	Unlimited enterprise grade apps for development

Table 5.3: SMP purchase options

It is important to understand that a purchase will have to be made if you consider upgrading in the future. Therefore, proper planning is essential when determining the long-term use of this environment.

5.2   SAP Service Marketplace

SAP will send an email outlining the download steps once a purchase is made. Please note this option is only for accessing the SMP Server. The SMP SDK download is addressed in Chapter 6.

SAP Service Marketplace

The SMP Server can be accessed from the URL in the Resources chapter. However, developers need to ensure that the account is associated as a developer in order to download the software. If the account is an **S** number, then contact SAP prior to making a purchase.

Exercise – SAP Service Marketplace

1. Log into the *SAP Service Marketplace* (link in Chapter 10)

2. Select SOFTWARE DOWNLOADS (see Figure 5.2)

3. Select the SUPPORT PACKAGES AND PATCHES TAB

4. Type sap mobile platform in the SEARCH TEXTBOX

SAP Software Download Center

Download SAP products that are associated with your S-User ID. You will require the *Download Software* authorization, which you can request via your company's SAP user administrator.

A subset of Analytics product patches is available without the need for an S-user logon.

Software Downloads	Download Basket	Application Overview and Help

Figure 5.2: SAP Marketplace Download Center

The next step is to download the appropriate package. Make sure to select the package which is compatible with the operating system.

Exercise – Installation product

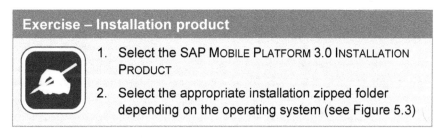

1. Select the SAP MOBILE PLATFORM 3.0 INSTALLATION PRODUCT

2. Select the appropriate installation zipped folder depending on the operating system (see Figure 5.3)

Selected Items (0)

Name	File Type
51048152 SAP Mobile Platform 3.0 Linux on x86_64 64bit	ZIP
51048153 SAP Mobile Platform 3.0 Windows on x64 64bit	ZIP
51046292 Agentry SAP Framework Foundation Windows 32/64B	ZIP

Figure 5.3: SMP server operating systems options

This zipped folder can be stored on the computer or server for installation.

SMP server installation tip

Refer to the SMP server installation link in Chapter 10 for additional information relating to operating system and requirements.

There are several databases you can use with the SMP server installation. The default database is *Derby*, but you have the option to use *ASE*, *DB2* or *Oracle*. However, these database instances need to be installed and configured prior to the SMP server installation. Refer to the SMP Installation guide in Chapter 10 if a database other than Derby is preferred.

5.3   SMP Server preparation

Prior to the installation ensure there is access to the Administration account and remove the Java Tools. Once the file has been downloaded, developers can start the process of installing SMP Server 3.0. The following exercise will take you through the setup and installation steps for the SMP Server.

Exercise – SMP server install

1. Download file
2. Create a new folder called SAP Mobile on Local Disk C
3. Extract contents of the zipped folder to the SAP MOBILE folder
4. Right click on *setup executable* and select SETUP AS ADMINISTRATOR. You may need to change the COMPATIBILITY to install SMP
5. Click NEXT on the WELCOME PAGE (see Figure 5.4)
6. Agree to the license, click NEXT
7. Select DEVELOPER or PRODUCTION INSTALLATION
8. Select the desired location to store the SMP Server file (see Figure 5.5)

The installation wizard will ask for certain selections such as the agreement to the license, development or production purpose, credentials to log into the server, operating system authentication and ports for configuration.

Figure 5.4: SMP Server install

Figure 5.5: SMP Server install location

Exercise – SMP server install continued...

9. Set KEYSTORE PASSWORD, ADMIN USER and ADMIN PASSWORD. Ensure to note the ADMIN USER NAME and PASSWORD CREDENTIALS – these values will be needed when logging into the SMP Server (see Figure 5.6)

10. Set SERVICE USER and PASSWORD for Windows (see Figure 5.7)

11. Set the PROTOCOL TYPE, identify the HOST NAME and identify the PORT: 8083 (see Figure 5.8)

12. Bypass the remaining steps

13. Click FINISH

Admin user and password tip

If this is for testing, you can use *smpAdmin* for the user name and *s3pAdmin* for the password.

SAP Mobile Platform Server 3.0

Enter the user name and password for the SAP Mobile Platform Cockpit admin user, and the password for accessing the keystore

Admin user name   smpAdmin

Admin password   •••••••••

Confirm admin password   •••••••••

Keystore password   •••••••••

Confirm keystore password •••••••••

< Back   Next >   Cancel

Figure 5.6: SMP Server admin user and password

SAP Mobile Platform Server 3.0

SAP Mobile Platform Server service configuration

☑ Start SAP Mobile Platform Server service automatically when Windows starts up

SAP Mobile Platform Server will run under a Windows User account, smpServiceUser.
Set a password for smpServiceUser User account. The password must meet the password policy
requirements, the minimum password length, password complexity and password history requirements.
If smpServiceUser account already exists on the system, enter password for smpServiceUser.

Windows account name: smpServiceUser

Windows account password: ●●●●●●●●●●

Confirm Windows account password: ●●●●●●●●●●|

< Back   Next >   Cancel

Figure 5.7: SMP Server operating systems username and password

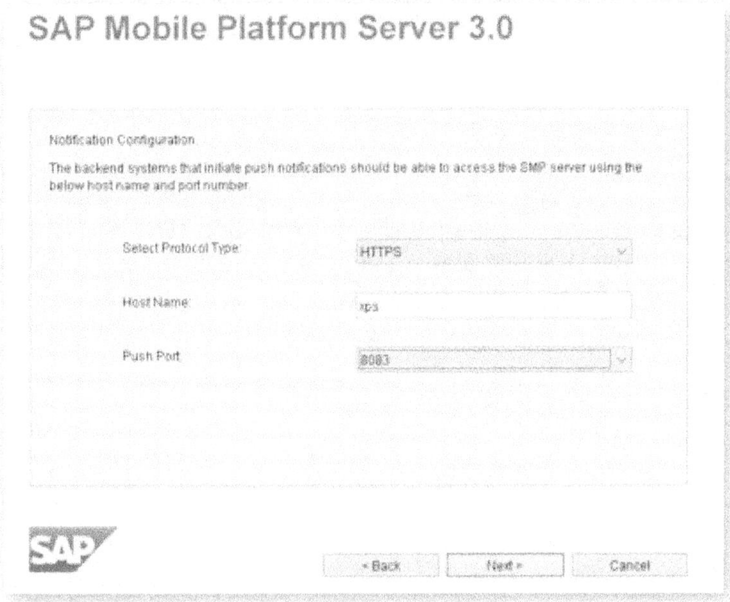

SAP Mobile Platform Server 3.0

Notification Configuration
The backend systems that initiate push notifications should be able to access the SMP server using the
below host name and port number.

Select Protocol Type: HTTPS

Host Name: xps

Push Port: 8083

< Back   Next >   Cancel

Figure 5.8: SMP Server notification configuration

The SMP Server is now installed. To start the services, click on the START SAP MOBILE icon on the desktop. This will start the server for administration and monitoring. It is also helpful to review the local services running on the machine. Review the *SAP Mobile Platform Server service* to ensure it is running. If the sevices are not running, click on the Restart option. Another option is to click back on the START SAP MOBILE icon on the desktop.

Exercise – Services

1. Go to SERVICES ON THE MACHINE (You may need to type services in the search for the operating system)

2. Find the SAP MOBILE PLATFORM SERVER SERVICE (see Figure 5.9)

3. Click START

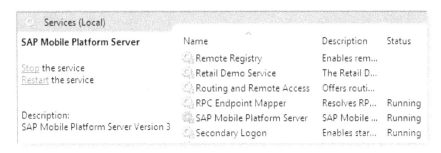

Figure 5.9: SMP Services

The final step to ensure that the installation was successful is to check the SAP Server login. The username and password entered in the installation wizard allows for the SMP server login.

Exercise – SMP Server login

1. Enter https://localhost:8083/Admin/ for the SMP SERVER URL

2. Enter the USER NAME

3. Enter the PASSWORD (see Figure 5.10)

4. Click LOG On

5. The Administration and Monitoring portal defaults to the HOME TAB (see Figure 5.11)

Figure 5.10: SMP Server login URL

Successful login authentication will open the *SMP Server Administration and Monitoring*. We will cover the HOME, APPLICATIONS, SETTING, REPORT-ING and LOGS tabs later in the chapter.

Figure 5.11: SMP Server Administration and Monitoring

5.4 Connect Eclipse to SAP Mobile Platform Administration and Monitoring

Eclipse Luna

New Eclipse versions such as *Neon* will be available in the future; however, at the time of writing this book, Luna is the only version that allows for both SAP Mobile Platform Tools and UI Development Toolkit for HTML5.

In Eclipse, let's complete the following steps to connect to the SAP Mobile Platform Administration and Monitoring portal:

Exercise – Eclipse connected to SMP Server

1. In Eclipse, Click on WINDOW • PREFERENCES • SAP MOBILE PLATFORM TOOLS • SERVER

2. Enter: https://localhost:8083 {Do not include the "/Admin/"}

3. USER: *********

4. PASSWORD: ******

5. Click TEST CONNECTION (see Figure 5.12)

This allows developers to connect an SAPUI5 app built with Eclipse to the SAP Mobile Platform Server. Once the application is built, the developer can right click and deploy the Eclipse project to the SMP Mobile Platform Server. It is important to note the differences between the SMP Server and SMP SDK.

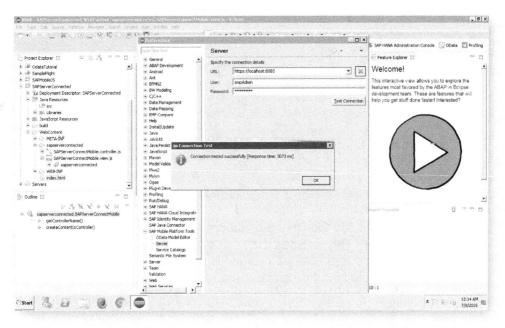

Figure 5.12: Eclipse connected to SMP Server

5.5 SMP Server new application

Let's take a look at a few options available with the SMP Server. Logically, the first step is to review the process for creating a new application.

Exercise – SMP Server login

1. Open a Browser

2. Type in https://localhost:8083/Admin/

3. Enter the USERNAME and PASSWORD

4. Click LOG ON

You'll see the following page (see Figure 5.13) once you have success-fully logged into the server.

Figure 5.13: SAP Mobile Platform Administration and Monitoring

The administration and monitoring portal provides many options to con-trol the application. This includes the *main dashboard, applications, set-tings, reporting* and logs. We will now focus on the new application pro-cess to demonstrate how this can be setup.

5.5.1 Application

Applications display the number of configurations in the platform. You can select the New button to create a new application. There are three options to select: *Native, Hybrid* and *Agentry*.

Exercise – New application
1. Click on the APPLICATIONS TAB   2. Click NEW   3. Click on the TYPE DROP DOWN BOX (see Figure 5.14)

Figure 5.14 shows the options to create a new app along with the application development types. The sections below describe the different options available for the new application.

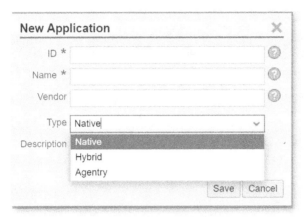

Figure 5.14: SMP Server New Application

Native

A native app is developed with Objective C for iOS, or Java for Android. Details for this development can be found in Chapter 1.

Hybrid

The ability to develop mobile apps utilizing HTML5, JavaScript and CSS. The advantages of this approach were reviewed in Chapter 1.

Agentry

Agentry is used for designing, developing, monitoring and deploying data-driven applications. The Admin UI allows developers to view applications, configure settings and observe logs. The Agentry client communicates with SMP using HTTPs and multiple database connections.

There are many beneficial features associated with the server. You have the ability to work on clusters, adjust the settings, analyze the reporting (see Figure 5.15) and review the logs. Although this is not the focus of this book, it is good to see how the server can integrate with SAPUI5 apps.

Figure 5.15: SMP Server reporting

5.6 Gateway Management Cockpit

Another tool available with the SMP Server install is the *SAP Gateway*. The SAP Gateway enables OData services to be used with the SAP Mobile Platform. This includes both SAP and non-SAP data sources. Developers can make Java Persistence API (JPA), Database and HTTP destinations. Let's take a quick look at the gateway as we finish the chapter. There are Integration Gateway Design Tools to build ODATA models with Eclipse. You can then export the OData to an SMP Server.

Exercise – SAP Gateway

1. Open a browser
2. Enter https://localhost:8083/gateway/cockpit
3. Enter the LOGIN CREDENTIALS from the installation steps
4. Click on DESTINATIONS
5. Click on CREATE
6. Review the DESTINATION TYPES (see Figure 5.16)

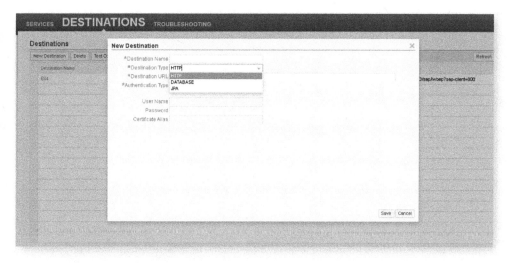

Figure 5.16: SMP Gateway

A data connection destination (see Figure 5.17) can be accessed through a hybrid development platform such as Eclipse. The Service Document link can be found in the overview of the service.

Figure 5.17: SMP Gateway destination

This environment can be beneficial especially if developing apps with Eclipse or the SAP Cloud Platform. There are options to deploy apps for both environments. This makes it advantageous to control apps with the administration and management portal.

6   SAP Mobile Platform SDK

The SMP SDK includes a variety of development options for mobile services and database connections. SMP SDK supports Apache Cordova and provides OData connectors. The SMP SDK offers many options to develop mobile apps using several development tools such as Native, Hybrid (Kapsel), Agentry (Meta driven) and SMS, with plugins and installs for Eclipse and Microsoft Visual Studio.

As discussed in Chapter 1, we have the opportunity to develop apps in a native or hybrid environment. The native approach focuses on one mobile operating system. This typically enables better testing because the emulator is designed to work strictly with the native Integrated Development Environment (IDE).

Figure 6.1 shows several options when developing mobile apps with the SMP SDK. The SAP Mobile SDK includes the *Agentry, Kapsel, Native, Fiori* and *SMS* toolkits for an assortment of development options.

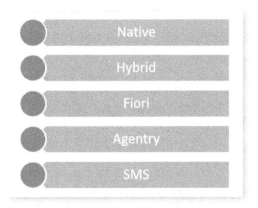

Figure 6.1: SMP SDK

There are several options available when installing the SMP SDK. The trial version is a free option that allows installation of the development SDKs.

Exercise – SMP SDK install

1. Log into the SAP Store and download the latest SMP SDK installer (see link in Chapter 10)

2. A download link to access a zipped file, which includes the setup executable, will be sent to your email address (see Figure 6.2)

3. RUN the executable file for the installation

Figure 6.2: SMP SDK download

SMP SDK download options

Make sure to first download the SDK Installer version before the upsidecar or PLO#. Note: you cannot install the PL01 or PL02 without first installing the SDK SP## Win or Mac version.

The installation is relatively easy to complete. There be may a need to adjust the compatibility and identify the file installation directory as performed with the SMP Server. Figure 6.3 shows the final progression of the SMP SDK installation.

Once the installation is complete, the SDKs and Toolkits shown in Figure 6.4 will be located on your computer. The Agentry, Kapsel and SDKs now reside on the machine. This is important especially when using Visual Studio for development with Kapsel. Visual Studio will need to locate the KapselSDK folder to enable the features associated with the plugin.

Figure 6.3: SMP SDK Installation Wizard

_smpjvm	5/11/2017 4:23 PM	File folder	
AgentryToolkit	5/11/2017 4:23 PM	File folder	
ClientHub	5/11/2017 4:21 PM	File folder	
InstallLogs	5/11/2017 4:19 PM	File folder	
KapselSDK	5/11/2017 4:22 PM	File folder	
NativeSDK	5/11/2017 4:21 PM	File folder	
SMSToolKit	5/11/2017 4:23 PM	File folder	
ThirdParty	5/11/2017 4:23 PM	File folder	
Tools	5/11/2017 4:21 PM	File folder	
Uninstaller	5/11/2017 4:23 PM	File folder	
smpsdk_product_info	5/11/2017 4:23 PM	XML Document	1 KB
smp-sdk-in-icon	6/19/2016 12:46 PM	Icon	32 KB

Figure 6.4: SMP SDKs and toolkits

As you can see, there are multiple toolkits and SDKs for development. This provides endless options to develop mobile apps. At this point, we have only installed the SMP SDK. We will review some of these options for development in the coming chapters.

6.1 SMP SDK for Visual Studio

There is another option for the SMP SDK install. We will work on SAPUI5 development with Visual Studio in Chapter 10, but it is now appropriate to show the SMP SDK install for Visual Studio. In this case, you are developing apps for the Fiori client using JavaScript instead of SAPUI5. However, it is good to know that this option is available should you have a need to build a Fiori app with Visual Studio (see Figure 6.6).

Exercise – SMP SDK for Visual Studio

1. Download the Installer (see Chapter 10 for link)
2. Select all SMP SDK OPTIONS (see Figure 6.5)
3. Click NEXT
4. Reboot the machine for the product to take effect
5. Open VISUAL STUDIO
6. Click FILE, NEW, PROJECT
7. Notice we now have an SAP OPTION under the JAVASCRIPT TEMPLATES (see Figure 6.6)

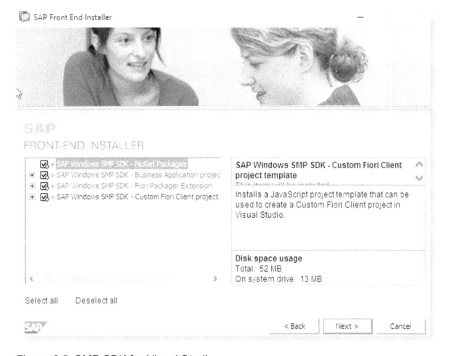

Figure 6.5: SMP SDK for Visual Studio

Figure 6.6: Visual Studio SAP Project

We have now completed the SMP SDK installations and stored all the toolkits and SDKs locally on our machines. This allows the development environments to locate the directory for each SDK when the time is appropriate. By installing the SMP Mobile Platform Server (Chapter 5) and SMP SDK (Chapter 6), we now understand the differences between the two environments and potential development opportunities using both. The next chapter will cover more on the SMP Server, especially with new applications and connections.

7 SAPUI5 with SAP Cloud Platform

The SAP Cloud Platform allows developers to use a cloud environment for developing, managing and deploying an array of applications. The SAP Cloud Platform has several options when it comes to developing applications in the environment. These options include Java, HTML5 and HANA XS Applications. Each provides feasible choices for building applications; however, this content focuses on HTML5 with the use of SAPUI5 for development.

7.1 Purchase options

The SAP Cloud Platform offers many purchase options. The options range from *developer* to *business* size, *starter* and *premium* editions. The focus of this content is on the developer edition because it is a logical step to explore the platform as decisions are made regarding the development environment. As with any environment, there should be proper planning to ensure the appropriate environment is deployed. Table 7.1 shows the basic options for each edition.

Platform	Free edition	Dedicated HANA instance	Production use
Developers	yes	yes, but with monthly subscription	no
Medium Business	yes	yes, but with monthly subscription	no
Enterprise	no	yes	no

Table 7.1: SAP Cloud Platform editions

Developer free edition tip

If this is your first time building apps with this environment, then it is recommended to use the trial Developer edition. You can then decide which paid edition is appropriate: Developer, Medium Business or Enterprise

The SAP Cloud Platform provides many categories for the cloud environment. Developers can view applications, services, connectivity, security and repositories along with many other options.

7.2 Logging into the SAP Cloud Platform

You need to establish an account with SAP before connecting to the cloud environment. This can be done by registering your SAP user account on the SAP Cloud Platform registration page (see Chapter 10).

User account tip

As a note, you can use the same SAP user account that was used in Chapter 5 for the SAP Mobile Platform download.

Let's complete the following to log into the SAP Cloud Platform:

Exercise – SAP Cloud Platform login

1. Go to sap.com
2. Click on the LOGON BUTTON
3. Click REGISTER if no account exists
4. Go to cloudplatform.sap.com
5. Register with your SAP user credentials

You now have access to the SAP Cloud Platform. There is an array of options so it is good to understand the features needed for app development. As seen in Figure 7.1, the initial overview will show the Java,

HTML5 and database systems active with your account. There are also options to review the services, persistence, connectivity, security, repositories and resource consumption. We will cover a few of these sections throughout this chapter.

Let's focus on the overview section. In this section, you can review the system status for Java, HTML5 and database systems. Note that this dashboard shows the applications, health status and database connections.

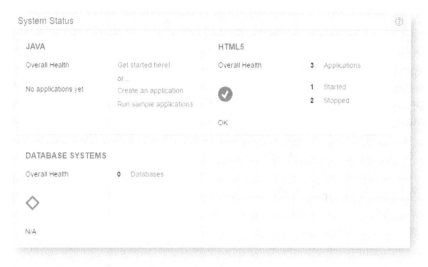

Figure 7.1: SAP Cloud Platform overview

7.2.1 Applications

Now that we have reviewed the overview dashboard for the platform, it's time to review the applications section. You will notice the options for Java, HTML5 and HANA XS. We want to briefly explore each, but the focus area here is with the use of HTML5 applications.

Java applications

As we discussed with Eclipse, the SAP Cloud Platform gives developers the option to create applications with the use of Java programming.

There are options in Eclipse that allow you to connect a Java-built app to the SAP Cloud environment. We will not cover this in a tutorial; you have to create a dynamic web project, run on the Java web server, and then modify the setting for the Hana On Demand host. This can be an advantageous strategy if you like developing apps with a native language such as Java, to be deployed to the SAP Cloud Platform. The ability to do this shows the flexibility and features available with the platform.

HTML5 applications

The overall goal of this book is to assist you to develop mobile apps using SAPUI5. This is the main focus for the development outlined in this chapter. At this point, it is critical to revisit the concepts learned in Chapter 1, covering HTML5, CSS, JavaScript and XML. Additionally, we will explore the Model View Controller (MVC) framework (see Chapter 3). The display shown in Figure 7.2 provides a snapshot of a few sample applications with an active state. The state provides a status of the application – whether it is running or not. As you can see, there are also options to create a new application and import existing zip files for the projects.

Figure 7.2: HTML5 applications

HANA XS applications

This application option is not covered in the development outlined in this book but it is good to know that the feature is available. HANA XS is an extended application service that provides the capability to embed application and web servers for building and deploying applications. This can certainly benefit developers when connecting to applications and databases.

7.2.2 Services

An important part of the platform is the *services* section. By clicking on the services, you can view and activate many categories for your application. Most of the services are relatively easy to activate by selecting a service and then enabling it. There are services for analytics, business, collaboration, data, development operations, integration, Internet of Things, mobile services, runtimes, security and user experience. A description of each service is provided under the selection option. We will use the SAP Web IDE (see Figure 7.3) for our SAPUI5 development.

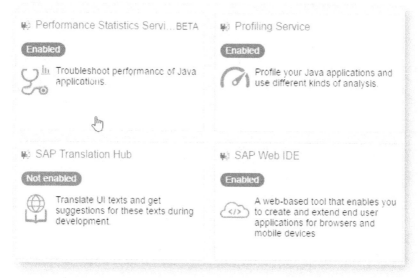

Figure 7.3: SAP Web IDE services

An example of one of the services is the *Internet of Things* (IoT), which provides the option to enable the service along with the description for its purpose. This service allows for the development of IoT applications. The example below shows the description for the IoT that can be found in the SAP Cloud Platform.

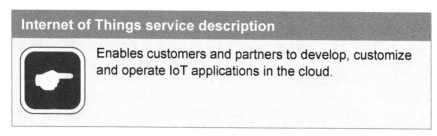

7.2.3 Persistence

The *persistence section* provides database systems, database schemas and service requests. Database systems show the state, database system and versions for the databases connected in the platform. Likewise, you find the schema ID, type, databases and versions in the schemas section. Service requests display information on the state, service, database system, requests and actions.

7.2.4 Connectivity

The *connectivity section* provides the ability to create the destinations and cloud connectors. Let's complete an activity in the connectivity section to add a database to the SAP Cloud Platform.

Exercise – Connect to an existing OData
1. Click on DESTINATIONS under CONNECTIVITY   2. Click on NEW DESTINATION   3. Type Northwind as the Name   4. Type Northwind OData Service as the Description   5. Type http://services.odata.org as the URL   6. Use the NOAUTHENICATION FOR AUTHENICATION   7. Click on NEW PROPERTY three times   8. Select WebIDEEnabled, true   9. Select WebIDESSystem, Northwind_Data   10. Select WebIDEUsage, odata_gen   11. Click SAVE

Figure 7.4 shows the fields for the exercise above.

We now have two options: to work on an existing configuration or to export the database. These options are found under the actions section in the Destinations screen. We will not perform any of these actions, but it is good to know about them in case such an activity is required. However, we can check the connection by clicking on the name of the database and selecting the check connection button.

Destination Configuration

* Name	Northwind
Type	HTTP ⌄
Description	Northwind OData Service
* URL	http://services.odata.org
Proxy Type	Internet ⌄
Authentication	NoAuthentication ⌄

Additional Properties   New Property

WebIDEEnabled	⌄	true	🗑
WebIDESystem	⌄	Northwind_Data	🗑
WebIDEUsage	⌄	odata_gen	🗑

Save   Cancel

Figure 7.4: Northwind destination

SAP Flight data

There are many tutorials and guides that use SAP Flight data for training. This is an excellent resource to explore before making connections to live data. Let's try another connection with the OData service provided by SAP.

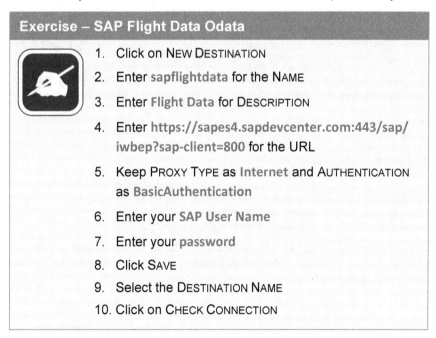

Exercise – SAP Flight Data Odata

1. Click on NEW DESTINATION
2. Enter sapflightdata for the NAME
3. Enter Flight Data for DESCRIPTION
4. Enter https://sapes4.sapdevcenter.com:443/sap/iwbep?sap-client=800 for the URL
5. Keep PROXY TYPE as Internet and AUTHENTICATION as BasicAuthentication
6. Enter your SAP User Name
7. Enter your password
8. Click SAVE
9. Select the DESTINATION NAME
10. Click on CHECK CONNECTION

Figure 7.5 shows the fields for the exercise.

Destination Configuration

* Name   sapflightdata
Type   HTTP
Description   Flight Data
* URL   https://sapes4.sapdevcenter.com:443/sap/iwbep?sap-client=800
Proxy Type   Internet
Authentication   BasicAuthentication
User
Password   ········

Additional Properties

No additional properties defined

✓ Use default JDK truststore

Figure 7.5: SAP Flight data destination

At this point, you should be successfully connected to the destination. We've now made the connections so we can move on to the security section of the SAP Cloud Platform.

7.2.5   Security

The *security section* of the platform provides options such as Trust, Authorizations and OAuth. We will not cover these features in this book, but it's useful to know there are security options for local service providers, application identity, platform identity, users, groups, branding, clients and APIs.

7.2.6   Repositories

In the *repository section*, we have options to explore documents or create Git clones. Git clones are populated into this section once you create the SAPUI5 app using the HTML5 Applications feature in the applications section. Figure 7.6 shows a sample of apps that have been created in the SAP Web IDE and then cloned with Git. We will perform the Git activity in Chapter 8.

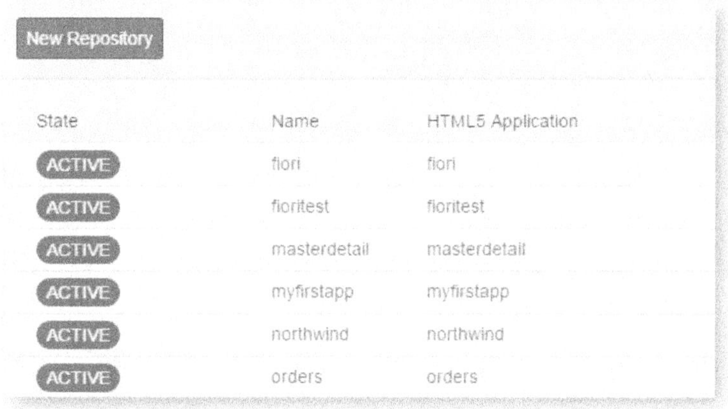

Figure 7.6: Git clones

7.2.7 Resource consumption

The last section we will cover is resource consumption. This section provides an overview of the different services you can use as well as the usage and total consumption. Please refer to Figure 7.7 for a snapshot of the features available.

Service	Usage Metric
Git	Fetch Count
	Push Count
	Repository Size
Network	Data Transfer
	Incoming Requests (HTML5 Applications)
Web IDE	Disk Usage

Figure 7.7: Resource consumption

We have now covered each of the sections in the SAP Cloud Platform Cockpit. It is helpful to review these options to see which features can be applied to your application as you develop.

8 Building Apps with the SAP Cloud Platform

The SAP Cloud Platform provides many opportunities when it comes to developing with Java or HTML5. As covered in Chapter 7, there are many supporting features to view services, analyze connectivity, inspect security and examine resource consumption when building apps in this platform. You will certainly find some of these features in other mobile development platforms, but not to this extent. In this chapter, we will focus on building mobile apps with the SAP Cloud Platform, but primarily with the SAP Web IDE, which is a service we reviewed in Chapter 7.

It is now time to build our first app in the SAP Cloud Platform. The framework will be similar to what we used in Eclipse, but this time we will use XML for the views instead of JavaScript.

8.1 Create app – SAP Cloud Platform

We want to start with the SAP Cloud Platform so we can view the app in SAP Web IDE. This is probably not the preferred approach, but it's good to examine the different options for development.

Exercise – New app

1. In the SAP CLOUD PLATFORM, select HTML5 APPLICATIONS under APPLICATIONS
2. Click on NEW APPLICATION (see Figure 8.1)
3. Name the application myfirstapp. Note: the application name has to be lower case.
4. Click SAVE
5. Under ACTIONS, click EDIT
6. Note the Clone Git Repository URL
7. Click CLONE
8. Click COMMIT AND PUBLISH

Figure 8.1: New HTML5 application

Git repository tip

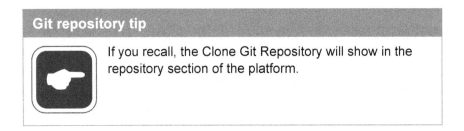

If you recall, the Clone Git Repository will show in the repository section of the platform.

We have now created an HTML5 app in the environment. You will see the app located under your workspace. In this example, we just want to demonstrate creating the app from the SAP Cloud Platform. This builds a shell inside the SAP Web IDE (see Figure 8.2). We now have the opportunity to create HTML, CSS, XML and JavaScript files for the project.

Figure 8.2: New application in workspace

This approach provides a blank framework in which to build the mobile app. However, it is probably best to utilize the SAPUI5 templates available in SAP Web IDE, which includes the MVC framework to build the apps. Let's move to the next section to create an app that utilizes an SAPUI5 template with the MVC framework.

8.2   Create app in SAP Web IDE

The previous exercise demonstrated the process of creating a basic application, but now we want to create our first SAPUI5 application. Complete the following exercise to utilize the template for this:

Exercise – SAP Web IDE new app

1. In the SAP WEB IDE, Click FILE, NEW, PROJECT FROM TEMPLATE

2. Click on the ALL CATEGORIES option under CATEGORIES

3. Select SAPUI5 APPLICATION (see Figure 8.3)

4. Click NEXT

5. Enter sapui5_mvc in the PROJECT NAME

6. Leave the NAMESPACE blank for now

7. Click NEXT

8. Use XML for the VIEW TYPE (see Figure 8.4)

9. Use View1 for the VIEW NAME

10. Click NEXT

11. Click FINISH

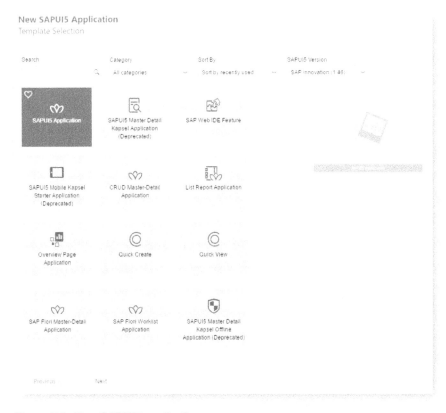

Figure 8.3: New SAPUI5 application

Figure 8.4: SAP Web IDE template customization

The new SAPUI5 app is now created. As we did with Eclipse, the first step is to review the file structure. Figure 8.5 displays the file structure with HTML, CSS, XML, Model and JavaScript files.

Figure 8.5: SAP Web IDE MVC files

The app uses the MVC framework with the model, view and controller. Please refer to Chapter 3 for detailed information on MVC. As noted before, we want to use the index page (Figure 8.6) to identify the SAP libraries, CSS and structure with the content for the views.

```
index.html  ×
 1   <!DOCTYPE HTML>
 2 ▾ <html>
 3
 4 ▾     <head>
 5             <meta http-equiv="X-UA-Compatible" content="IE=edge" />
 6             <meta charset="UTF-8">
 7
 8             <title>sapui5_mvc</title>
 9
10 ▾         <script id="sap-ui-bootstrap"
11                 src="../../resources/sap-ui-core.js"
12                 data-sap-ui-libs="sap.m"
13                 data-sap-ui-theme="sap_belize"
14                 data-sap-ui-compatVersion="edge"
15                 data-sap-ui-resourceroots='{"sapui5_mvc": ""}'>
16         </script>
17
18         <link rel="stylesheet" type="text/css" href="css/style.css">
19
20 ▾     <script>
21 ▾         sap.ui.getCore().attachInit(function() {
22 ▾             new sap.m.Shell({
23 ▾                 app: new sap.ui.core.ComponentContainer({
24                         height : "100%",
25                         name : "sapui5_mvc"
26                     })
27                 }).placeAt("content");
28             });
29         </script>
30     </head>
31
32 ▾     <body class="sapUiBody" id="content">
33     </body>
34
35 </html>
```

Figure 8.6: Index page

8.2.1 Model

Next, we need to review the model. In the `model.js`, notice the one-way binding for the *oModel*. This provides the data logic for the files. Figure 8.7 displays the code for the `model.js`.

```
 1 ▾ sap.ui.define([
 2        "sap/ui/model/json/JSONModel",
 3        "sap/ui/Device"
 4 ▾ ], function(JSONModel, Device) {
 5        "use strict";
 6
 7 ▾     return {
 8
 9 ▾         createDeviceModel: function() {
10              var oModel = new JSONModel(Device);
11              oModel.setDefaultBindingMode("OneWay");
12              return oModel;
13          }
14
15      };
16 });
```

Figure 8.7: SAPUI5 model.js

8.2.2 View

The view provides the content the user will see when viewing the app. As shown in Table 8.1, we need the resourceroots to search for the controller, controller.extend to gather the content from *View1*, and controllerName in *View1* to identify the controller for this view.

Page	Code
index.html	data-sap-ui-resourceroots
View1.view.xml	controllerName= "sapui5_mvc.controller.View1"
View1.controller. js	Controller.extend("sapui5_mvc.controller. View1"

Table 8.1: MVC for index, view, controller

Let's now make a few modifications to the view. To change the title of the initial page, we have to modify the View1.view.xml.

Exercise – Update <Page> tag

1. In the `View1.view.xml`, update the `<Page>` tag to `<Page title="My SAPUI5 App">` (see Figure 8.2)

2. Save the page (example: ⌷Ctrl⌷ + ⌷S⌷)

```
index.html ×    models.js ×    View1.view.xml ×
 1 ▾ <mvc:View controllerName="sapui5_mvc.controller.View1" xmlns:html="http://www.w3.org/1999/xhtml
 2       displayBlock="true" xmlns="sap.m">
 3 ▾      <App>
 4 ▾        <pages>
 5 ▾          <Page title="My SAPUI5 App">
 6              <content></content>
 7            </Page>
 8          </pages>
 9        </App>
10    </mvc:View>
```

Figure 8.8: View1 title

We can run the app to ensure the title has been changed, but let's add a *VBox* and *Grid* before doing so.

VBox tip

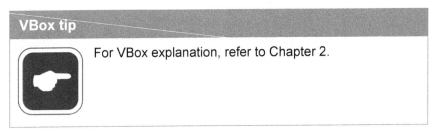

For VBox explanation, refer to Chapter 2.

Exercise – VBox and grid

1. Open the `View1.view.xml` page if it is not already open

2. Within `<content> </content>` script, add the code shown in Listing 8.1

3. Save the file

```
<content>

    <VBox width="100%" direction="Column" id="__vbox0">
        <items>
            <sap.ui.layout:Grid xmlns:sap.ui.layout="sap.ui.layout" id="__grid0">
```

```
<sap.ui.layout:Grid xmlns:sap.ui.layout="sap.ui.layout" id="__grid0">
    <sap.ui.layout:content>
        <ObjectListItem title="cloud" number="10"  intro="Services" icon="sap-icon://cloud" id="__item0"/>
        <ObjectListItem title="database" number="5"  intro="Services" icon="sap-icon://database" id="__item1"/>
        <ObjectListItem title="web-cam" number="7"  intro="Services" icon="sap-icon://web-cam" id="__item2"/>
    </sap.ui.layout:content>
</sap.ui.layout:Grid>
```

```
            </sap.ui.layout:Grid>
        </items>
    </VBox>
```

```
</content>
```

Listing 8.1: Code for inside content tag

8.2.3 Controller

As discussed above, controllers are used by the views. For example, if a *View1* view is created, you use the `View1.js` controller with the associated view. Figure 8.9 outlines the code for the controller. Please note the *controller extend code statement* for *View1*.

```
sap.ui.define([
    "sap/ui/core/mvc/Controller"
], function(Controller) {
    "use strict";

    return Controller.extend("helloworld.controller.View1", {
        handleListItemPress: function(evt) {
            var oRouter = sap.ui.core.UIComponent.getRouterFor(this);
            var selectedProductId = evt.getSource().getBindingContext().getProperty("ProductID");
            oRouter.navTo("detail", {
                productId: selectedProductId
            });
        }

    });

});
```

Figure 8.9: View controller

We can now run the app because we have updated View1.

Exercise – Preview app
1. Click on the `index.html` page 2. Click on the RUN button (see Figure 8.10) 3. View the app in the browser (see Figure 8.11)

Figure 8.10: Run app

Figure 8.11: App output

You can now modify some of the code in the View1 page. Remember, you can use the *SAPUI5 Development Kit* (see Chapter 10) to help make the adjustments. It is good to adjust the *ObjectListItem* title, *number* and *icon*. You can click on the ICON tab (see Figure 8.12) in the SAP DEVELOPMENT KIT to see a list of available icons.

105

Figure 8.12: SAPUI5 Development Kit icons

Exercise – On your own

1. On your own. Go back to the `View1.view.xml` and change the code inside the `<content>` tag

2. Rerun the app to see the changes

8.3   Layout Editor

The Layout Editor, in the SAP Web IDE, is extremely attractive for developing apps. We have seen this with many web and mobile app development environments. It gives developers the opportunity to look at the layout while building an app.

Exercise – Layout Editor

1. In the SAP WEB IDE, select FILE, NEW, QUICK START WITH LAYOUT EDITOR (see Figure 8.13)

2. For the APPLICATION NAME enter `QuickStartApplication`

3. Open the `View1.view.xml`

4. RIGHT CLICK on `View1.view.xml` and select OPEN WITH, LAYOUT EDITOR (see Figure 8.14)

5. Observe the layout in the `View1.view.xml` (see Figure 8.15)

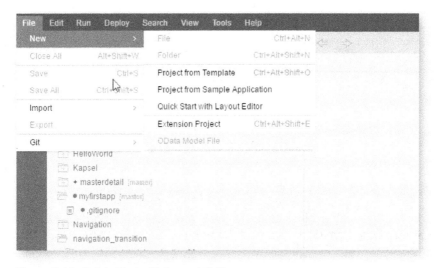

Figure 8.13: Quick Start with Layout Editor

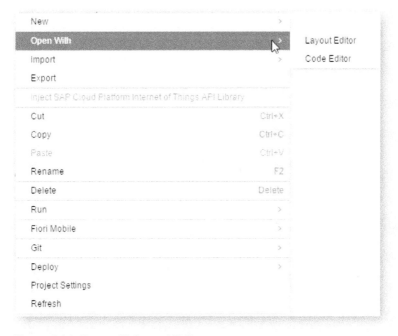

Figure 8.14: Open with Layout Editor

Figure 8.15: View with Layout Editor

You now have the opportunity to view the *Action*, *Container*, *Display*, *Layout*, *List*, *Semantic*, *Tile* and *User Input* controls in the CONTROLS SECTION, as seen in Figure 8.16.

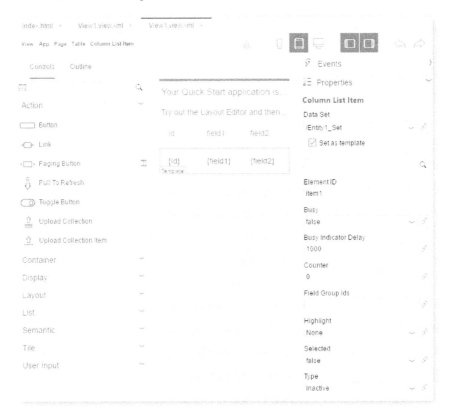

Figure 8.16: Layout Editor properties

108

The controls shown in Figure 8.17 coincide with the SAPUI5 Development Toolkit discussed in Chapter 2. Additionally, you can see the correlation with the *sap.m library* under the OUTLINE SECTION that was also discussed in Chapter 2. Therefore, as we build the app with the Layout Editor we can also verify and review our practices with the SAP Development Toolkit.

Figure 8.17: Layout Editor controls and outline

This provides many opportunities to construct the layout of the app by dragging the controls to the canvas. Each time you bring on a new control and click save, these changes are applied to the code of the `View1.view.xml`.

8.4   Odata app

Building an app that is data-driven is important and valuable, especially with business apps. In this tutorial, we want to use the Northwind destination that we previously created in the connectivity section (see Chapter 7). We can use these settings to develop our first data-driven application. Figure 8.18 lists the available destinations in the Destination section of the SAP Cloud Platform.

Destinations (All: 4)

New Destination   Import Destination   Certificates

Type	Name	Basic Properties		Actions
HTTP	Northwind	Authentication	NoAuthentication	
		ProxyType	Internet	
		URL	http://services.odata.org	
HTTP	Northwind_d	Authentication	NoAuthentication	
		ProxyType	Internet	
		URL	http://services.odata.org	
HTTP	sapflightdata	Authentication	BasicAuthentication	
		ProxyType	Internet	
		URL	https://sapes4.sapdevcenter.com:443/sap/	
HTTP	SAPServer	Authentication	BasicAuthentication	
		ProxyType	Internet	
		URL	https://H/sap01-205.ides.consolut.com/S/6;	

Figure 8.18: Database destinations

Exercise – Northwind OData Service

1. In the SAP WEB IDE, Click FILE, NEW, FROM TEMPLATE

2. Select ALL CATEGORIES from the CATEGORY OPTION

3. Select SAPUI5 MASTER DETAIL KAPSEL APPLICATION (see Figure 8.19)

4. Type Orders for the PROJECT NAME

5. Click NEXT

6. Select the SERVICE URL from SOURCES

7. Select the NORTHWIND ODATA SERVICE that was created in the DESTINATIONS SECTION

8. Type /V2/northwind/northwind.svc

9. Click on the TEST BUTTON (see Figure 8.20)

10. Click NEXT

11. Type com.orders.database for the PROJECT NAMESPACE (see Figure 8.21)

12. Type Orders for the MASTER SECTION TITLE

13. Enter Orders_Details in the ODATA COLLECTION

14. Enter Find in the SEARCH PLACEHOLDER

15. Enter Orders in the SEARCH TOOLTIP

16. Enter OrderID in the SEARCH FIELD

17. Enter OrderID in ITEM TITLE

18. Select Quantity in NUMERIC ATTRIBUTE

19. Select UnitPrice for UNITS ATTRIBUTE

20. Enter Order Details for TITLE

21. Select OrderID in ADDITIONAL ATTRIBUTE1

22. Select ProductID in ADDITIONAL ATTRIBUTE2

23. Select Product for ODATA NAVIGATIONS

24. Select ProductName for NAVIGATION ATTRIBUTE1

25. Select UnitPrice for NAVIGATION ATTRIBUTE2

26. Select UnitsInStock for NAVIGATION ATTRIBUTE3

27. Click NEXT

28. FINISH

Use Version 2 in Step 8

It is important to note that you have to use Version 2 in Step 8 to retrieve the data from the Northwind database.

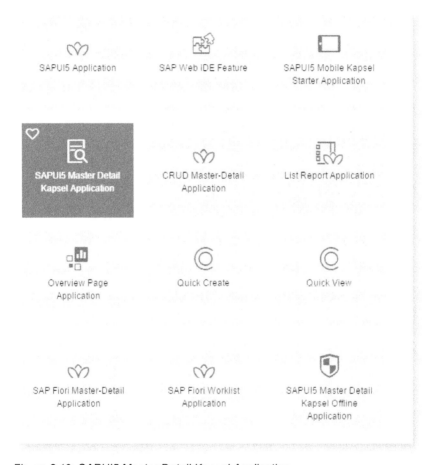

Figure 8.19: SAPUI5 Master Detail Kapsel Application

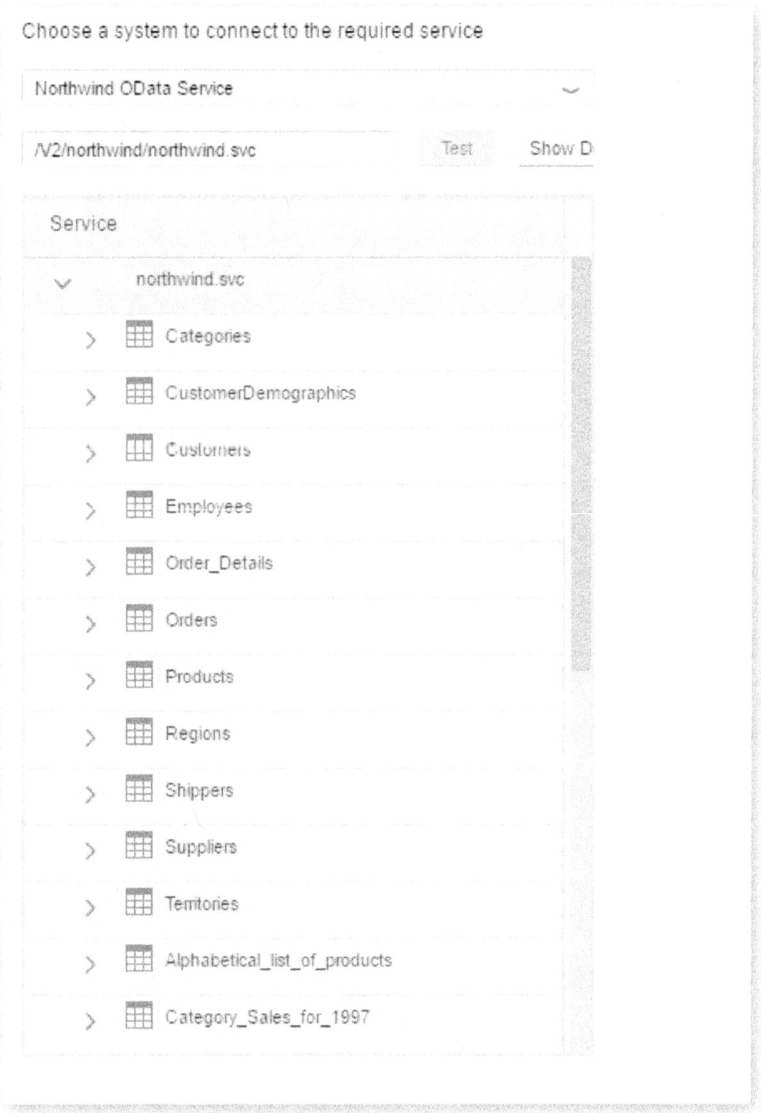

Choose a system to connect to the required service

Northwind OData Service

/V2/northwind/northwind.svc   Test   Show D

Service

northwind.svc

> Categories

> CustomerDemographics

> Customers

> Employees

> Order_Details

> Orders

> Products

> Regions

> Shippers

> Suppliers

> Territories

> Alphabetical_list_of_products

> Category_Sales_for_1997

Figure 8.20: Northwind OData Service

New SAPUI5 Master Detail Kapsel Application
Template Customization

Project Settings	Project Namespace	com.orders.database	
Master Section	Title	Orders	
	OData Collection*	Order_Details	⌄
	Search Placeholder	Find	
	Search Tooltip	Orders	
	Search Field	OrderID	⌄
Main Data Fields	Item Title	OrderID	⌄
	Numeric Attribute	Quantity	⌄
	Units Attribute	UnitPrice	⌄
Detail Section	Title	Order Details	
	Additional Attribute 1	OrderID	⌄
	Additional Attribute2	ProductID	⌄
Information Sec...	OData Navigations	Product	⌄
	Navigation Attribute1	ProductName	⌄
	Navigation Attribute2	UnitPrice	⌄
	Navigation Attribute3	UnitsInStock	⌄

Figure 8.21: Project settings

The Northwind OData application has been created. We now need to open the index.html page. The code looks different to our previous examples because we now have to get parameters and additional functions to load the data from the database.

1. Open `index.html` page

2. Run the application

3. Review and explore the ORDERS and ORDER DETAILS for the app (see Figure 8.22)

Figure 8.22: Order Details output

You can use the navigation at the top to review the orders and investigate the details by clicking on the specific order. It is good to see how this works so that you can apply the database connection concept to an SAP server or OData connection.

8.5 Create, import, route and deploy app

Let's work on a new app that creates a shell, imports from SAP Development Kit and deploys back to the SAP Cloud Platform.

Exercise – Create folder and download source

1. In the SAP WEB IDE, right click on the WORKSPACE FOLDER, select FOLDER

2. Enter import_route_deploy as the FOLDER NAME

3. Click OK

4. Go to the SAP DEVELOPMENT TOOLKIT (see Chapter 10)

5. Click on the DEVELOPER GUIDE TAB

6. Click on NAVIGATION AND ROUTING

7. Click on STEP 8: NAVIGATION WITH FLIP TRANSITION

8. Click on the ROUTING AND NAVIGATION LINK – you can download this template within the Coding section on the page (see Figure 8.23)

9. Click on the SHOW SOURCE FOR SAMPLE icon (see Figure 8.24)

10. Click on the DOWNLOAD link

11. Save the zipped folder to a location on your hard drive

Figure 8.23: SAPUI5 Development Toolkit Navigation download link

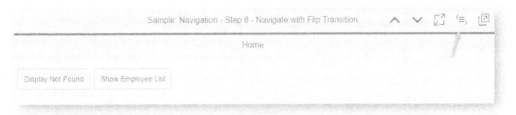

Figure 8.24: Routing and Navigation download code

Exercise – Import

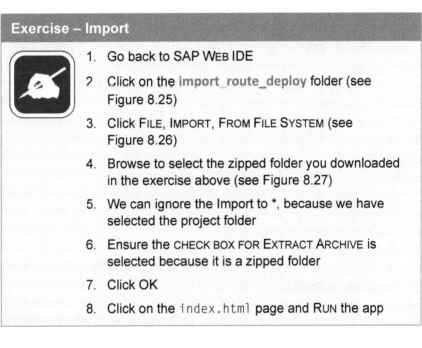

1. Go back to SAP WEB IDE

2. Click on the import_route_deploy folder (see Figure 8.25)

3. Click FILE, IMPORT, FROM FILE SYSTEM (see Figure 8.26)

4. Browse to select the zipped folder you downloaded in the exercise above (see Figure 8.27)

5. We can ignore the Import to *, because we have selected the project folder

6. Ensure the CHECK BOX FOR EXTRACT ARCHIVE is selected because it is a zipped folder

7. Click OK

8. Click on the index.html page and RUN the app

Figure 8.25: Import_route_deploy folder

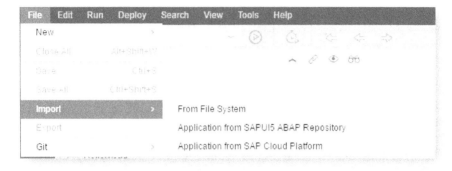

Figure 8.26: File, Import, From File System

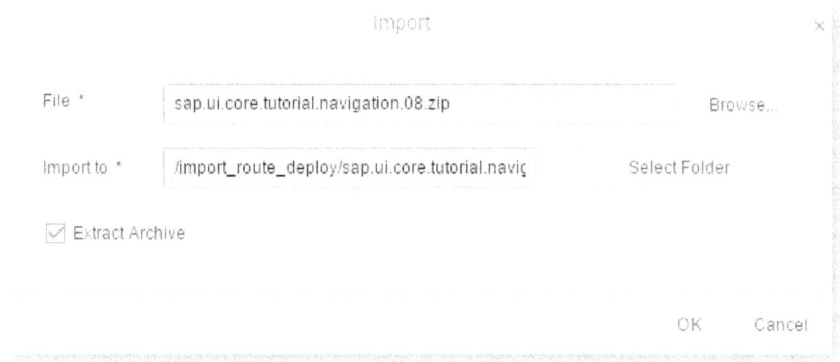

Figure 8.27: Import folder

We have imported the SAP Development Toolkit tutorial folder for this exercise. You will see that the file structure is very similar to what we have been working with previously. Figure 8.28 displays the file structure for the tutorial files. It is a best practice to copy the webapp, JavaScript, HTML and JSON files to the main `import_route_deploy` folder. You can then delete the `sap.ui.core.tutorial.navigation.08` folder so the file alignment is consistent with the SAPUI5 framework.

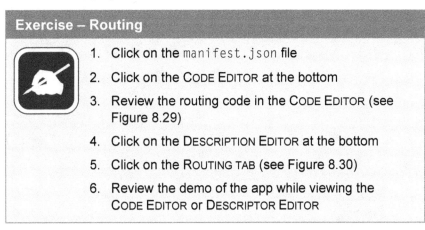

📂 import_route_deploy
  📂 sap.ui.core.tutorial.navigation.08
    📂 webapp
      📁 controller
      📁 i18n
      📁 localService
      📁 view
      📄 Component.js
      📄 index.html
      📄 manifest.json

Figure 8.28: File structure

Let's take a look at the routing of this app. We have two options when it comes to creating or modifying the routing of the app. These options are the *Code Editor* or *Descriptor Editor*. As we did with the Layout Editor, we can use the form fields to add the routing or hard code the routing in the Code Editor. In this particular scenario, the routing goes to a page not found or an employee list.

Exercise – Routing

1. Click on the `manifest.json` file

2. Click on the CODE EDITOR at the bottom

3. Review the routing code in the CODE EDITOR (see Figure 8.29)

4. Click on the DESCRIPTION EDITOR at the bottom

5. Click on the ROUTING TAB (see Figure 8.30)

6. Review the demo of the app while viewing the CODE EDITOR or DESCRIPTOR EDITOR

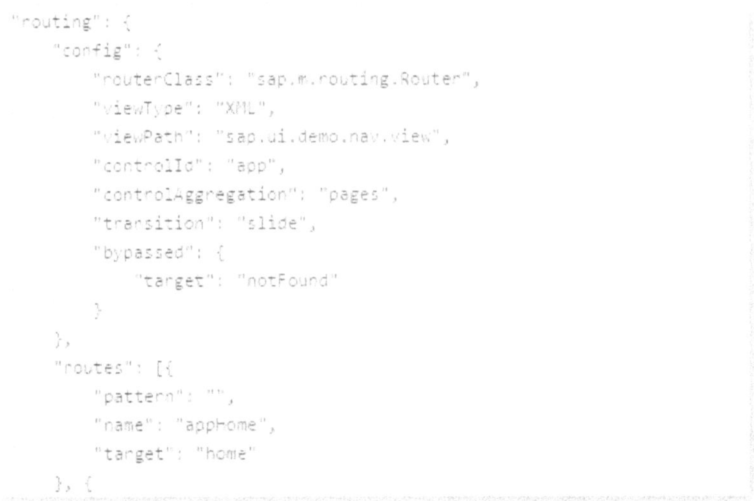

```
"routing": {
    "config": {
        "routerClass": "sap.m.routing.Router",
        "viewType": "XML",
        "viewPath": "sap.ui.demo.nav.view",
        "controlId": "app",
        "controlAggregation": "pages",
        "transition": "slide",
        "bypassed": {
            "target": "notFound"
        }
    },
    "routes": [{
        "pattern": "",
        "name": "appHome",
        "target": "home"
    }, {
```

Figure 8.29: Routing Code Editor

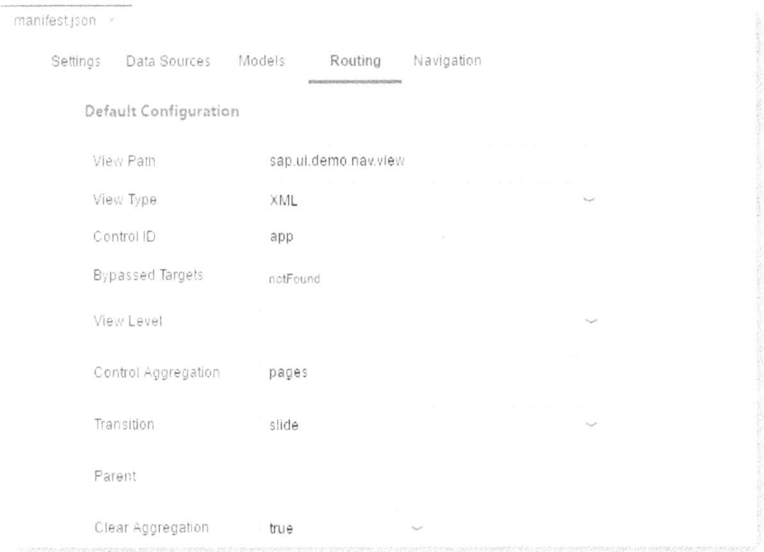

manifest.json

Settings   Data Sources   Models   Routing   Navigation

Default Configuration

View Path	sap.ui.demo.nav.view	
View Type	XML	⌄
Control ID	app	
Bypassed Targets	notFound	
View Level		⌄
Control Aggregation	pages	
Transition	slide	⌄
Parent		
Clear Aggregation	true	⌄

Figure 8.30: Routing Descriptor Editor

In this section, we have imported an app and reviewed the routing. We can now deploy the app back to our SAP Cloud Platform. There are several options when it comes to deploying the app. These options include: deploying to SAPUI5 ABAP Repository, SAP Cloud Platform, register to SAP Fiori Launchpad, and Hybrid App Toolkit (Local Add-On). For now, let's use the `import_route_deploy` application to deploy the app to the SAP Cloud Platform.

Exercise – Deploy app

1. Before deployment, go back to the SAP CLOUD PLATFORM

2. Click on HTML5 APPLICATIONS UNDER APPLICATIONS

3. Review your existing applications

4. Go back to the SAP WEB IDE

5. Right click on the import_route_deploy folder

6. Click DEPLOY

7. Select DEPLOY TO SAP CLOUD PLATFORM (see Figure 8.31)

8. Review the Deploy Settings (see Figure 8.32)

9. Click DEPLOY

10. Click CLOSE on the SUCCESSFULLY DEPLOYED MESSAGE (see Figure 8.33)

Figure 8.31: Deploy app to SAP Cloud Platform

Figure 8.32: Deploy settings

Successful deployment means the app is now available in the SAP Cloud Platform.

Figure 8.33: Successful deployment to SAP Cloud Platform

It is time to go back to the SAP Cloud Platform to review the deployed app.

Exercise – Review deployed app

1. Go back to the SAP Cloud Platform
2. Click on HTML5 APPLICATIONS
3. Notice the app is now listed as *Started* in the APPLICATION LIST (see Figure 8.34)

Figure 8.34: Deployed app

8.6 Git clone app

The application shows as Started because we have just deployed it from the SAP WEB IDE. You can always click on the STOP icon under ACTIONS to stop the app. You can then restart it by clicking on the START icon. Let's go back to the SAP Web IDE by clicking on EDIT APPLICATION under ACTIONS.

Exercise – Git clone

1. Click on EDIT APPLICATION under ACTIONS
2. Review the Git URL
3. Click on CLONE (see Figure 8.35)

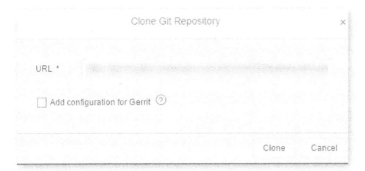

Figure 8.35: Clone Git Repository

Exercise – Commit

1. Click COMMIT AND PUSH (see Figure 8.36)
2. Notice the "Clone has been completed" message at the top of the SAP WEB DIE

Figure 8.36: Git Ignore Systems Files

8.7 Delete app

There will be times when you have to delete an app from the SAP Web IDE or SAP Cloud Platform. Let's go back to the first app that we created with the SAP Cloud Platform. This was a test app so we can delete it from our workspace.

Exercise – SAP Web IDE delete app

1. RIGHT CLICK on the project folder
2. Select DELETE (see Figure 8.37)
3. Click OK on the CONFIRMATION NEEDED DIALOG BOX
4. The app has been deleted

Figure 8.37: SAP Web IDE delete app

The app was deleted from the SAP Web IDE, but it still exists in the SAP Cloud Platform.

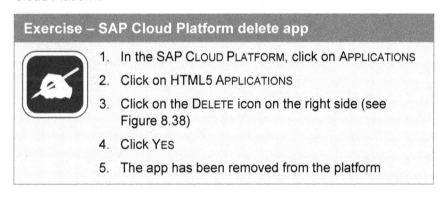

Figure 8.38: SAP Cloud Platform delete app

The SAP Cloud Platform is very useful. It provides many opportunities for building and controlling the services, data connections, security and repositories. The SAP Web IDE service is terrific; it enables SAPUI5 development, offers many templates and supports the Layout Editor for the controls. This environment already offers so much, but we will see more tools and available features in the coming years.

9 Building SAPUI5 Apps with Visual Studio

We have discussed various opportunities when it comes to developing apps with SAPUI5. We now enter the last development environment for developing with SAPUI5. Microsoft Visual Studio is usually used to develop business applications with C# or Visual Basic. However, with the integration of Cordova and Visual Studio, developers have the ability to build web or mobile applications using HTML, CSS and JavaScript. Visual Studio also offers the opportunity to use the Kapsel SDK and SMP SDK to build Fiori apps.

One advantage of Visual Studio is that this environment now offers a community version and not only professional or enterprise editions. There are some limitations to the community version, including limited testing tools, debugging and diagnostics, and cross-platform development. The cross-platform development limitation does not interfere with our development for SAPUI5 apps. It is recommended to download the Community edition to see how SAPUI5 can be utilized. You can then purchase the professional or enterprise version.

Download tip

Download the latest Visual Studio community version. The versions are usually released every two years.

The first thing we need to do is download the Visual Studio community edition. You will notice that Microsoft has done a better job to support additional programming languages such as HTML, JavaScript, Type-Script and Python in its IDE. The strategy to include these programming languages may be a little late, but at least Microsoft is reaching out to other communities and developers to use the Visual Studio environment.

The approach here is to build a hybrid app using Visual Studio with Cordova and SAPUI5. As we did before, we will again use HTML5, CSS and JavaScript as we build the application.

Cordova tip

Visual Studio 2015 requires you to download the Cordova framework. This can be done by selecting the Online sections and then searching for Cordova in the Search textbox. This framework takes several minutes to install. You will then have the JavaScript Installed templates on your machine for development.

Exercise – Visual Studio download

1. Click on the DOWNLOAD VS COMMUNITY LINK VS 2017 (see Chapter 10)

2. RUN the exe file

3. Select YES for the install

4. Select MOBILE DEVELOPMENT WITH JAVASCRIPT (See Figure 9.1)

5. Click INSTALL (note: the system may require a restart)

6. Open VISUAL STUDIO

7. Login with your Microsoft account

8. Select DEVELOPMENT SETTINGS

9. Select the desired theme

10. Click START VISUAL STUDIO

Mobile development with JavaScript
Build Android, iOS and UWP apps using Tools for Apache Cordova

Figure 9.1: Mobile development with JavaScript

9.1 New project

We now have the platform ready so we can create our first project using Visual Studio.

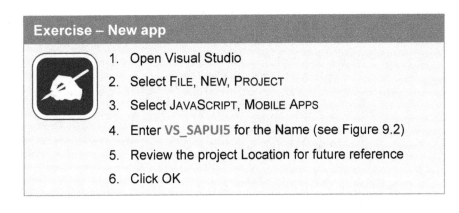

Exercise – New app

1. Open Visual Studio
2. Select FILE, NEW, PROJECT
3. Select JAVASCRIPT, MOBILE APPS
4. Enter **VS_SAPUI5** for the Name (see Figure 9.2)
5. Review the project Location for future reference
6. Click OK

Figure 9.2: New project

Let's examine the code as we did with Eclipse and SAP Cloud Platform. Open the index.html page (see Figure 9.3) under the www folder. You will notice that the HTML structure is different to that used with the other SAPUI5 pages. There are several references to Cordova and scripts for building the mobile app. However, we have to make a few adjustments for the structure to use SAPUI5.

```
<!DOCTYPE html>
<html>
    <head>
        <!--
            Customize the content security policy in the meta tag below as needed. Add 'unsafe-inline' to default-src
            For details, see http://go.microsoft.com/fwlink/?LinkID=617521
        -->
        <meta http-equiv="Content-Security-Policy" content="default-src 'self' data: gap: https://ssl.gstatic.com
        <meta http-equiv="content-type" content="text/html; charset=UTF-8" />
        <meta name="format-detection" content="telephone=no">
        <meta name="msapplication-tap-highlight" content="no">
        <meta name="viewport" content="user-scalable=no, initial-scale=1, maximum-scale=1, minimum-scale=1, width
        <link rel="stylesheet" type="text/css" href="css/index.css">
        <title>VSSAPUI5</title>
    </head>
    <body>
        <div class="app">
            <h1>Apache Cordova</h1>
            <div id="deviceready" class="blink">
                <p class="event listening">Connecting to Device</p>
                <p class="event received">Device is Ready</p>
            </div>
        </div>
        <script type="text/javascript" src="cordova.js"></script>
        <script type="text/javascript" src="scripts/platformOverrides.js"></script>
        <script type="text/javascript" src="scripts/index.js"></script>
    </body>
</html>
```

Figure 9.3: HTML code with Cordova

There are numerous options we can choose for apps that use Cordova plug-ins. You can access the Cordova plug-ins by opening the `config.xml` file and clicking on the PLUG-INS option. We will not utilize these plug-ins in this book, but it is good to see how easy it is to install a particular plug-in to your app structure. Figure 9.4 shows the Plugins section on the `config.xml` file. Additionally, Chapter 1 covers possible Cordova plugins that can be utilized with the apps.

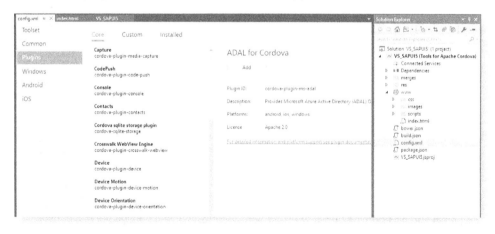

Figure 9.4: Cordova plugins

As mentioned above, our app is not quite ready to run in the simulator with our SAPUI5 code. We now need to modify the index.html page to support the SAPUI5 framework.

Exercise – Open UI5 code to app

1. Go to http://openui5.org/
2. Click on DOWNLOAD
3. Click on DOWNLOAD OPENUI5 RUNTIME
4. Save the zipped folder to your computer
5. Extract the zipped folder
6. Copy the RESOURCES folder
7. Open the VS_SAPUI5 APP in Visual Studio
8. Right click on the project name VS_SAPUI5(Tools for Apache Cordova) and select PASTE
9. Expand the RESOURCES folder to review the controls

Paste resource folder tip

You may need to close out the solution and reopen if the paste is not working.

Note the common sap-m files that were reviewed in Chapter 2. Figure 9.5 outlines some of the controls that can be used for development.

Figure 9.5: sap.m controls

Now that we have our support libraries in place under the resource folder, we can adjust the index page to support the SAPUI5 development.

Exercise – Modify index page

1. Open the `index.html` page
2. Remove the existing HTML and Cordova code
3. Add the code from Figure 9.6 to the index page

```
index.html*  ⇄  ×  config.xml
    1       <!DOCTYPE html>
    2       <html xmlns="http://www.w3.org/1999/xhtml">
    3       <head>
    4           <title></title>
    5           <script id="sap-ui-bootstrap"
    6                   src="resources/sap-ui-core.js"
    7                   data-sap-ui-theme="sap_bluecrystal"
    8                   data-sap-ui-libs="sap.m"></script>
    9           <script>
   10
   11               var oButton1 = new sap.m.Button({
   12                   text: "Button",
   13                   tooltip: "This is a test tooltip",
   14                   press: function () { alert('Alert from ' + oButton1.getText()); }
   15               });
   16               // attach it to some element in the page
   17               oButton1.placeAt("content");
   18
   19           </script>
   20       </head>
   21       <body class='sapUiBody'>
   22           <div style="margin:100px;">
   23               <div id='content'></div>
   24           </div>
   25       </body>
   26       </html>
   27
```

Figure 9.6: Modified index page

We are now ready to run the app in the simulator. The great thing about this particular simulator is that you can select from LG, Nexus, Galaxy and other devices. You also have the option to install Android build tools and emulators with the Run options. This gives developers more options for testing the devices for the app.

Exercise – Run simulator

1. Click on the SIMULATOR RUN command next to ANDROID (see Figure 9.7)
2. It will take several seconds before the simulator displays the output
3. Click on the OK button to view the ALERT (see Figure 9.8)

Figure 9.7: Run command

Figure 9.8: Simulator output

9.2 Kapsel

An advancement in mobile development is the opportunity to build native applications without limitations from the browser. There are a variety of examples available with SAP Fiori library. As you recall, we installed SAP Mobile SDK, which included the *Kapsel SDK*. The SAP Mobile SDK was installed in Chapter 6. The Kapsel SDK was in the installation.

Kapsel is a set of SAP plugins for Apache Cordova, to enable development of hybrid applications (SAP, 2013). Kapsel includes *App Update, Auth Proxy, Encrypted Storage, Logger, Logon, Push* and *Settings plugins*, as seen in Table 9.1. In order to use Kapsel, a Cordova app has to be created. This can be done with Eclipse for Android or Xcode for iOS. You can then upload the Kapsel app to SMP Administration and Monitoring (see Chapter 5).

Login Manager	Offline OData	Push
App Update	Logger	E2E Tracing
Settings	Auth Proxy	Barcode Scanning
Calendar	Encrypted Storage	Voice Recording
In-App Message	App Preferences	Attachment Viewer
Printer	Online Apps	Toolbar

Table 9.1: Kapsel SDK

Exercise – Verify Kapsel SDK

1. Locate your SMP SDK that was installed in Chapter 6
2. Click on the KAPSELSDK folder
3. Ensure the files were installed (see Figure 9.9)

This PC › Local Disk (C:) › SAP › MobileSDK3 › KapselSDK › plugins

	Name	Date modified	Type
	apppreferences	5/11/2017 4:22 PM	File folder
	appupdate	5/11/2017 4:21 PM	File folder
	attachmentviewer	5/11/2017 4:21 PM	File folder
	authproxy	5/11/2017 4:21 PM	File folder
	barcodescanner	5/11/2017 4:22 PM	File folder
	cachemanager	5/11/2017 4:22 PM	File folder
	calendar	5/11/2017 4:22 PM	File folder
	cdsprovider	5/11/2017 4:22 PM	File folder
	corelibs	5/11/2017 4:22 PM	File folder
	e2etrace	5/11/2017 4:22 PM	File folder
	encryptedstorage	5/11/2017 4:21 PM	File folder
	federationprovider	5/11/2017 4:22 PM	File folder
	fioriclient	5/11/2017 4:22 PM	File folder
	i18n	5/11/2017 4:22 PM	File folder
	inappbrowser	5/11/2017 4:22 PM	File folder
	inappbrowser-xwalk	5/11/2017 4:22 PM	File folder
	logger	5/11/2017 4:21 PM	File folder
	logon	5/11/2017 4:22 PM	File folder

Figure 9.9: Kapsel SDK

Let's create a project that will identify the Kapsel plugins.

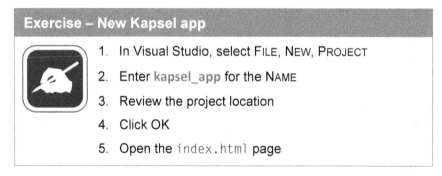

Exercise – New Kapsel app

1. In Visual Studio, select FILE, NEW, PROJECT
2. Enter kapsel_app for the NAME
3. Review the project location
4. Click OK
5. Open the index.html page

As we have seen before, the index.html page in Visual Studio is different to our SAPUI5 template applications. We will not adjust the index.html code, but we need to create the config.json page so we can activate the Kapsel plugins.

Exercise – Create config.json

1. Right click on the KAPSEL_APP (Tools for APACHE CORDOVA) folder
2. Select ADD, NEW ITEM
3. Enter config.json as the FILE NAME (see Figure 9.10)

Figure 9.10: Create config.json file

We now need to modify the config file to search for the Kapsel SDK on the machine.

Exercise – Modify config.json

1. Open the config.json
2. Remove the existing code
3. Add the code located in the example below (Note: ensure the Kapsel SDK is in this location. If not, then make the adjustment to the file path)
4. SAVE the file

config.json code example

```
{
        "plugin_search_path":
"C:\\SAP\\MobileSDK3\\KapselSDK\\plugins\\"
}
```

Exercise – Install Kapsel plugin

1. Open the `config.xml` (not the config.json file)
2. Click on PLUGINS
3. Click on CUSTOM
4. Select the LOCAL RADIO button
5. Click on the BROWSE icon
6. Locate the KAPSEL SDK on the machine.
7. Drill down to the PLUGINS folder (see Figure 9.11)
8. Click on the VOICERECORDING folder
9. Click OK
10. Click ADD
11. Note the PLUGINS folder on your SOLUTION EXPLORER (see Figure 9.12)

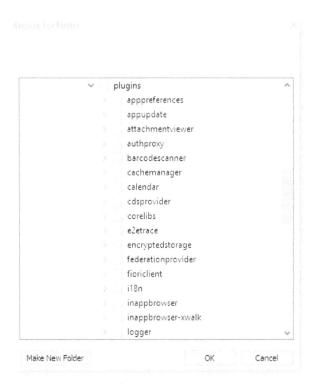

Figure 9.11: Browse for Kapsel plugin

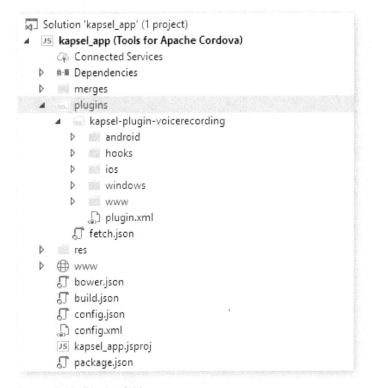

Figure 9.12: Plugins folder

We have another option when it comes to adding plugins.

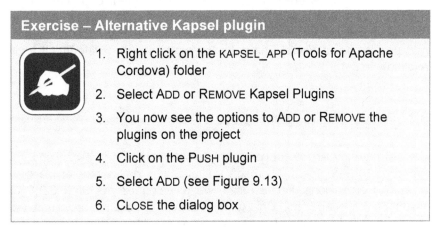

Exercise – Alternative Kapsel plugin

1. Right click on the KAPSEL_APP (Tools for Apache Cordova) folder

2. Select ADD or REMOVE Kapsel Plugins

3. You now see the options to ADD or REMOVE the plugins on the project

4. Click on the PUSH plugin

5. Select ADD (see Figure 9.13)

6. CLOSE the dialog box

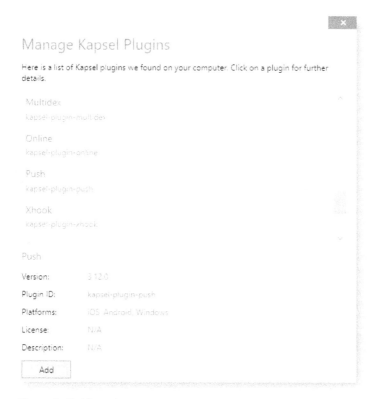

Figure 9.13: Kapsel Push plugin

The intent here is to show how we can use the SAP tools integrated within the Visual Studio environment. This provides great opportunities for building robust and data-driven apps with functionality that can be seen on most mobile applications. Therefore, we significantly boost the quality and usefulness of Visual Studio by having all these development tools available to us.

9.3   Visual Studio market place

We will now investigate several further options that can assist and improve our development. Microsoft Visual Studio has a market place to download extensions. If you recall, we downloaded the SMP SDK for Visual Studio extension in Chapter 6. However, we are not only limited to this particular extension. There are options for SAP ODBC Driver, Data Flow and Open UI5.

9.4 Git

There may be times when you need to import templates or project samples into Visual Studio. To do this, you need to install the Git extension for Visual Studio.

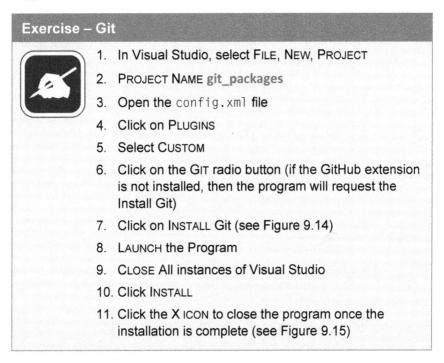

Exercise – Git

1. In Visual Studio, select FILE, NEW, PROJECT
2. PROJECT NAME git_packages
3. Open the config.xml file
4. Click on PLUGINS
5. Select CUSTOM
6. Click on the GIT radio button (if the GitHub extension is not installed, then the program will request the Install Git)
7. Click on INSTALL Git (see Figure 9.14)
8. LAUNCH the Program
9. CLOSE All instances of Visual Studio
10. Click INSTALL
11. Click the X ICON to close the program once the installation is complete (see Figure 9.15)

Figure 9.14: Install Git

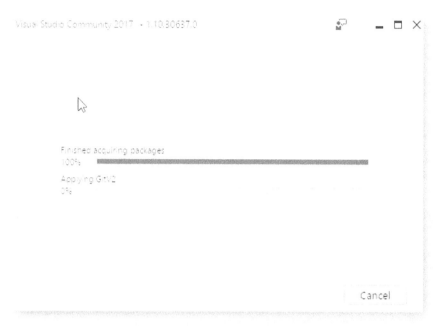

Figure 9.15: Installing Git

We now have the GitHub extension installed so we can go back to the project. The next exercise will allow us to retrieve the GIT repository using the `config.xml file`.

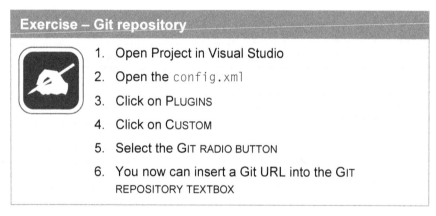

9.5   OpenUI5-sources

Let's continue with the same project so we can investigate a few more packages.

Exercise – Bower package

1. Right click on the GIT_PACKAGES (Tools for Apache Cordova) folder

2. Click on MANAGE BOWER PACKAGES

3. Click on the BROWSE option

4. Type SAP in the SEARCH TEXT FIELD

5. Search for OPENUI5-SOURCES package

6. Click INSTALL

7. The plugin will be installed to the environment (see Figure 9.16)

8. Review the BOWER_COMPONENTS folder with openui5-sources (see Figure 9.17)

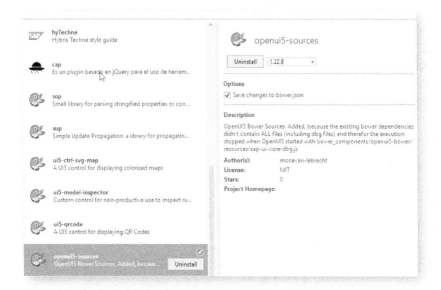

Figure 9.16: OpenUI5-sources

This is similar to what we saw when we pasted the *Open UI5 Resources* folder into the project earlier in this chapter. Figure 9.17 shows the libraries for sap.m in the project file structure. We need to modify the *index.html page* to utilize these controls.

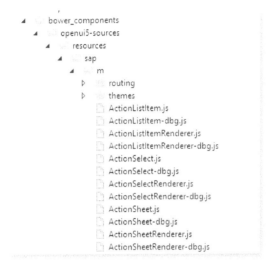

Figure 9.17: sap.m library under bower_components

As you can see, there are many options to build mobile apps with Visual Studio. We can build apps using SAPUI5 using Open UI5 packages, Kapsel with the Kapsel SDK and Cordova, and Fiori with the SMP SDK for Visual Studio. This gives us options to meet customers' demands and requirements for business apps.

10 Resources

The resources identified in the chapters of this book can be found via the following links:

- ▶ Eclipse Download: *https://www.eclipse.org/downloads/?*
- ▶ Open UI5: *http://openui5.org/*
- ▶ SAP Cloud Platform Registration: *https://www.sap.com/developer/tutorials/hcp-create-trial-account.html*
- ▶ SAP Service Marketplace: *https://websmp201.sap-ag.de/*
- ▶ SAP Mobile Platform: *https://www.sap.com/products/mobile-app-development-platform.html*
- ▶ SAP Mobile Platform SDK: *https://store.sap.com/sap/cp/ui/resources/store/html/SolutionDetails.html?pid=0000013098&catID=&pcntry=US&sap-language=EN&_cp_id=id-1409756206625-0*
- ▶ SMP SDK for Visual Studio: *https://marketplace.visualstudio.com/items?itemName=SAPSE.SAPMobilePlatformSMPSDKforWindows*
- ▶ SAPUI5 Development Toolkit: *https://sapui5.hana.ondemand.com/#docs/guide/95d113be50ae40d5b0b562b84d715227.html*
- ▶ SMP Server Installation Tips: *https://help.sap.com/doc/download_multimedia_zip-smp_install_win_smp_server_installation_win_pdf/3.0.3/en-US/smp_server_installation_win.pdf*
- ▶ Visual Studio Community Download: *https://www.visualstudio.com/vs/community/*
- ▶ Visual Studio Editions: *https://www.visualstudio.com/vs/compare/*
- ▶ Visual Studio GitHub Extension: *https://visualstudio.github.com/*
- ▶ Visual Studio SMP SDK for Windows: *https://marketplace.visualstudio.com/items?itemName=SAPSE.SAPMobilePlatformSMPSDKforWindows*

11 References

► SAP (2013). *Mobile Application Development for Developers*

► SAP (2014). *Native OData App Development Using the OData API.*

You have finished the book.

A   The Author

Figure 11.1: Robert Burdwell Ph.D.

Robert Burdwell is an Assistant Professor with Texas: A&M University, San Antonio and ERP Consultant with Burcamp. He has extensive experience in website and software development, system analysis, database integration, enterprise resource planning systems and business intelligence. He continually works with several organizations to improve their website development and online operations.

As for his education, he has a BS in Business Administration, MS in Computer Information Systems and a Ph.D. in Business with a focus on Information Technology Management. He has many certifications: Project Manager Professional (PMP), Certified Ethical Hacker (CEH), Titanium Certified App Developer (TCAD), Microsoft Certified Professional, Web Developer (ASP.Net and Adobe) and Database Programming.

To keep his information technology knowledge up to date, he participates in software development projects, attends technology conferences and training courses, and conducts research in the areas of enterprise resource planning and project management. He also enjoys volunteering with the Project Management Institute (PMI) and networking with professional organizations.

B   Index

A
Agentry 63

C
Cordova 18, 130
CSS 12, 14

E
Eclipse 43, 62, 77

H
HTML 13
HTML5 12, 13, 96

I
IDE 79
Internet of Things 89

J
Java 87

K
Kapsel 63, 135

M
MVC 33

O
OData 18, 57, 60, 115
OpenUI5 22

S
SAP Cloud Platform 77, 85, 95
SAP Gateway 76
SAP Mobile 61
SAP Mobile SDK 79
SAP Mobile Server Toolkit 57
SAP Web IDE 97, 106
SAPUI5 21, 22, 81, 97, 132
security 92
SMP 3.0 62, 64
SMP Mobile Platform Server 83
SMP SDK 64, 79, 83
SMP Server 66, 70, 76
SMP Server Administration and
   Monitoring 71

V
Visual Studio 127

X
XML 16

C Disclaimer

This publication contains references to the products of SAP SE.

SAP, R/3, SAP NetWeaver, Duet, PartnerEdge, ByDesign, SAP BusinessObjects Explorer, StreamWork, and other SAP products and services mentioned herein as well as their respective logos are trademarks or registered trademarks of SAP SE in Germany and other countries.

Business Objects and the Business Objects logo, BusinessObjects, Crystal Reports, Crystal Decisions, Web Intelligence, Xcelsius, and other Business Objects products and services mentioned herein as well as their respective logos are trademarks or registered trademarks of Business Objects Software Ltd. Business Objects is an SAP company.

Sybase and Adaptive Server, iAnywhere, Sybase 365, SQL Anywhere, and other Sybase products and services mentioned herein as well as their respective logos are trademarks or registered trademarks of Sybase, Inc. Sybase is an SAP company.

SAP SE is neither the author nor the publisher of this publication and is not responsible for its content. SAP Group shall not be liable for errors or omissions with respect to the materials. The only warranties for SAP Group products and services are those that are set forth in the express warranty statements accompanying such products and services, if any. Nothing herein should be construed as constituting an additional warranty.

More Espresso Tutorials Books

Michal Krawczyk:

SAP® SOA Integration – Enterprise Service Monitoring

- ► Tools for Monitoring SOA Scenarios
- ► Forward Error Handling (FEH) and Error Conflict Handler (ECH)
- ► Configuration Tips
- ► SAP Application Interface Framework (AIF) Customization Best Practices
- ► Detailed Message Monitoring and Reprocessing Examples

http://5077.espresso-tutorials.com

Anurag Barua:

First Steps in SAP® Fiori

- ► SAP Fiori fundamentals and core components
- ► Instructions on how to create and enhance an SAP Fiori app
- ► Installation and configuration best practices
- ► Similarities and differences between SAP Fiori and Screen Personas

http://5126.espresso-tutorials.com

Paul Bakker & Rick Bakker:

How to Pass the SAP® ABAP Certification Exam

► Essential guide on how to pass the ABAP Associate Certification exam

► Expert ABAP certification tips

► Overview of certification exam topics

► Short and full-length practice exams with answer guides

http://5136.espresso-tutorials.com

Thomas Stutenbäumer:

Practical Guide to ABAP®. Part 2: Performance, Enhancements, Transports

► Developer influence on performance

► Modifications and enhancements to SAP standard

► SAP access and account management techniques

► SAP Transport Management System

http://5138.espresso-tutorials.com

Bert Vanstechelman:

The SAP® HANA Deployment Guide

▶ SAP HANA sizing, capacity planning guidelines, and data tiering

▶ Deployment options and data provisioning scenarios

▶ Backup and recovery options and procedures

▶ Software and hardware virtualization in SAP HANA

http://5171.espresso-tutorials.com

Raquel Seville:

SAP® OpenUI5 for Mobile BI and Analytics

▶ Delve into the foundations of CSS, HTML5, and jQuery

▶ Learn how to build a seamless mobile BI app using SAP OpenUI5

▶ Use open source library d3.js to create custom data visualizations for bar, line, and pie charts

▶ Build web apps using real world scenarios and test layout options for different mobile devices

http://5173.espresso-tutorials.com

www.ingramcontent.com/pod-product-compliance
Lightning Source LLC
LaVergne TN
LVHW022321060326
832902LV00020B/3590